SAY IT IN
MODERN GREEK

BY

GEORGE PAPPAGEOTES, Ph.D.

Lecturer in Modern Greek

COLUMBIA UNIVERSITY

NEW YORK

DOVER PUBLICATIONS, INC.

Say It in Greek is a new work, first published by Dover
Publications, Inc., in 1956.

International Standard Book Number: 0-486-20813-3

Manufactured in the United States of America
Dover Publications, Inc., 31 East 2nd Street, Mineola, N.Y. 11501

SCHEME OF PRONUNCIATION

The sound system of Greek is easy to master. It has only five vowels (similar to those of Spanish):

a as in *father*, which is transcribed by *ah* or *a*,
e as in *met*, which is transcribed by *eh* or *e*,
i as in *machine*, which is transcribed by *ee*,
o as in *obey*, which is transcribed by *oh* or *o*, and
u as *oo* in *fool*, which is transcribed by *oo*.

Its consonants appear in English with the exception of χ, which is like *ch* in the German *ich* and *ach* and in that Scottish *loch* (lake) and is transcribed by *kh*; and of γ (the voiced counterpart of χ), which before *i* and *e* is like English *y* as in *yes* and is transcribed by *y* and before *a*, *o*, and *u* is pronounced as the English *g* in *go*, but continued, and is transcribed by *gh*. The *th* as in *thin* is transcribed by *th*, but the *th* as in *those* is transcribed as *th̲*. The rest of the consonants have the same sound value that they have in English. Accented (i.e. stressed) syllables are written in capitals.

The orthography of the Greek text is based on that used and recommended in the *Grammar of Modern Greek* (Νεοελληνικὴ Γραμματικὴ, Ο.Ε.Σ.Β., Athens, 1941), written by a committee appointed by the Minister of Education of Greece.

The abbreviations *m.*, *f.*, and *n.* stand for masculine, feminine, and neuter respectively, and they indicate that the use of the gender of the article or of the adjective depends on the gender of the noun which they modify.

Above all, this book tries to reflect the linguistic reality of present-day Greek.

THE GREEK ALPHABET

The Greek alphabet has twenty-four letters.

CHARACTER		NAME		PRONOUNCED
Α	α	Ἄλφα	AL-fa	as *a* in *fa*ther
Β	β	Βῆτα	VEE-ta	as *v* in *v*est
Γ	γ	Γάμμα	GHA-ma	as *y* in *y*es or as *gh*, the voiced counterpart of *ch* in the Scottish lo*ch*
Δ	δ	Δέλτα	THEL-ta	as *th* in *th*ose
Ε	ε	Ἔψιλον	EP-see-lohn	as *e* in l*e*t
Ζ	ζ	Ζῆτα	ZEE-ta	as *z* in *z*est
Η	η	Ἦτα	EE-ta	as *ee* in f*ee*
Θ	θ	Θῆτα	THEE-ta	as *th* in *th*ink
Ι	ι	Ἰῶτα	YO-ta	as *ee* in f*ee**
Κ	κ	Κάππα	KA-pa	as *k* in *k*ing
Λ	λ	Λάμβδα	LAM-tha	as *l* in *l*ift
Μ	μ	Μῦ	MEE	as *m* in *m*iss
Ν	ν	Νῦ	NEE	as *n* in *n*o
Ξ or Ζ	ξ	Ξῖ	KSEE	as *ks* in si*x*
Ο	ο	Ὄμικρον	O-mee-krohn	as *o* in *o*bey
Π	π	Πῖ	PEE	as *p* in *p*ut
Ρ	ρ	Ρῶ	RO	as *r* in *r*oll
Σ	σ (-ς)	Σῖγμα	SEEGH-ma	as *s* in *s*ea or *z* before *m* or any other voiced consonant as in *z*est
Τ	τ	Ταῦ	TAF	as *t* in *t*en
Υ	υ	Ὕψιλον	EEP-see-lohn	as *ee* in f*ee*
Φ	φ	Φῖ	FEE	as *f* in *f*ee
Χ	χ	Χῖ	KHEE	as *ch* in the Scottish lo*ch*
Ψ	ψ	Ψῖ	PSEE	as *ps* in ti*ps*
Ω	ω	Ὠμέγα	o-MEGH-ah	as *o* in *o*bey

* The letter ι is pronounced as *y* in *y*es in colloquial Greek after a consonant (and especially after the sonants m, n, l, and r) and before a vowel.

USEFUL EXPRESSIONS

1. Yes. No. Perhaps.
Ναί. Ὄχι. Ἴσως.
neh. O-khee. EE-sohss.

2. Please.
Παρακαλῶ.
pa-ra-ka-LO.

3. Excuse me.
Συγγνώμην.
seeg-NO-meen.

4. Help me.
Βοηθῆστέ με.
vo-ee-THEE-stem-eh.

5. Thanks (very much).
Εὐχαριστῶ (παρὰ πολύ).
ef-kha-ree-STO (pa-ra-po-LEE).

6. You are welcome.
Παρακαλῶ.
pa-ra-ka-LO.

7. Does anyone here speak English?
Εἶναι κανείς ἐδῶ ποὺ νὰ μιλᾶ ἀγγλικά;
*EE-neh kah-NEESS eh-$\overline{THO}$ poo na mee-LAH
ahn-glee-KA?*

8. I speak only English (French).
Μιλῶ μόνον ἀγγλικά (γαλλικά).
mee-LO MO-nohn ahn-glee-KA (gha-lee-KA).

9. I know a little German (Italian, Spanish).

Ξέρω λίγα γερμανικά (ἰταλικά, ἰσπανικά).

KSEH-ro LEE-gha yer-mah-nee-KA,
  (ee-ta-lee-KA, ee-spah-nee-KA).

10. I am an American citizen.

Εἶμαι ἀμερικανὸς πολίτης.

EE-meh ah-meh-ree-ka-NOHSS po-LEE-teess.

11. I do not understand.

Δὲν καταλαβαίνω.

THEN ka-ta-la-VEH-no.

12. Repeat it, please.

Πέστε το πάλι, παρακαλῶ.

PEH-steh-toh PA-lee, pa-ra-ka-LO.

13. Write it down, please.

Γράψτε το, παρακαλῶ.

GHRAH-psteh-toh, pa-ra-ka-LO.

14. The address.

Ἡ διεύθυνσις.

ee thee-EF-theen-seess.

15. The date.

Ἡ ἡμερομηνία.

ee ee-meh-ro-mee-NEE-ah.

16. The number.

Ὁ ἀριθμός.

oh ah-reeth-MOHSS.

17. The time.

Ὁ χρόνος.

oh KHRO-nohss.

18. How do you say ——?
Πῶς λέτε ——;
POHSS LEH-teh ——?

19. What is this called in Greek?
Πῶς τὸ λένε αὐτὸ ἑλληνικά;
POHSS toh-LEH-neh af-TOH eh-lee-nee-KA?

20. My name is ——.
'Ονομάζομαι or μὲ λένε ——.
o-no-MA-zo-meh or meh-LEH-neh ——.

21. I spell my name ——.
Γράφω τὸ ὄνομά μου με ——.
GHRA-fo toh-O-no-MA-moo meh——.

22. My (mailing) address is ——.
'Η (ταχυδρομικὴ) διεύθυνσή μου εἶναι ——.
*ee (ta-khee-thro-mee-KEE) thee-EF-theen-see-
moo EE-neh ——.*

23. Please speak more slowly.
Παρακαλῶ μιλᾶτε πιὸ ἀργά.
pa-ra-ka-LO mee-LA-teh PYO ar-GHA.

24. What do you wish?
Τί θέλετε;
TEE THEH-leh-teh?

25. Where is? or Where are?
Ποῦ εἶναι;
POO EE-neh?

26. Wait a moment.
Περιμένετε μιὰ στιγμή.
peh-ree-MEH-neh-teh mee-ΛΗ stee-GHMEE.

27. How much is it?
Πόσο ἔχει;
POH-so EH-khee?

28. It is old (new).
Εἶναι παλιὸ (καινούργιο).
EE-neh pa-LYO (keh-NOOR-yo).

29. It is (not) all right.
(Δὲν) εἶναι ἐν τάξει.
(then) EE-neh en-DA-ksee.

30. That is (not) all.
Αὐτὸ (δὲν) εἶναι ὅλο.
ahf-TOH (then) EE-neh OH-lo.

31. Why? Γιατί; *ya-TEE?*

32. When? Πότε; *PO-teh?*

33. How? Πῶς; *POHSS?*

34. How far? Πόσο μακρυά;
POH-so mah-kree-AH?

35. How long? Πόσον καιρό;
POH-sohn geh-RO?

36. Who? Ποιός *m.,* ποιά *f.*
pee-OHS? pee-AH?

37. What? Τί; *TEE?*

38. Here. 'Εδῶ. *eh-THOH.*

39. There. 'Εκεῖ. *eh-KEE.*

40. From. 'Από. *ah-PO.*

41. With. Μέ. *meh.*

42. Without. Χωρίς. *kho-REES.*

43. To the. or **In the.**
Στό(ν) *m.*, στή(ν) *f.*, στό *n.*
stoh(n). stee(n). sto.

44. Near. Κοντά. *kohn-DA.*

45. Far. Μακρυά. *ma-kree-AH.*

46. In front of. Μπροστά. *broh-STA.*

47. Behind. Πίσω. *PEE-so.*

48. Beside. Δίπλα. *T͞HEE-pla.*

49. Inside. Μέσα. *MEH-sa.*

50. Outside. Ἔξω. *EH-kso.*

51. Something. Κάτι. *KAH-tee.*

52. Nothing. Τίποτε. *TEE-po-teh.*

53. Several. Κάμποσα. *KAHM-bo-sa.*

54. Few. Λίγα. *LEE-gha.*

55. Many. Πολλά. *po-LA.*

56. Enough. Ἀρκετά. *ahr-keh-TAH.*

57. Too much. Παρὰ πολύ. *pa-ra-po-LEE.*

58. (Much) more, less.
(Πολὺ) περισσότερο, λιγότερο.
(po-LEE) peh-ree-SO-teh-ro, lee-GHO-teh-ro.

59. Empty. Ἄδειο. *AH-t͞hee-o.*

60. Full. Γεμάτο. *yeh-MA-toh.*

61. Good. Καλό. *ka-LO.*

62. Better (than). Καλύτερο (ἀπό).
ka-LEE-teh-ro (ah-PO).

63. (the) Best. Τὸ καλύτερο.
to ka-LEE-teh-ro.

64. Bad. Κακό. *ka-KO.*

65. Worse (than). Χειρότερο (ἀπό).
khee-RO-teh-ro (ah-PO).

66. (the) Worst. Τὸ χειρότερο.
toh-khee-RO-teh-ro.

67. Again. Πάλι. *PA-lee.*

68. Also. Ἐπίσης. *eh-PEE-seess.*

69. Now. Τώρα. *TOR-ah.*

70. Immediately. Ἀμέσως. *ah-MEH-sohss.*

71. As soon as possible.
Ὅσο τὸ δυνατὸν γρηγορώτερα.
OH-so toh-thee-na-TOHN ghree-gho-RO-teh-ra.

72. Soon. Σύντομα. *SEEN-doh-ma.*

73. Later. Ἀργότερα. *ahr-GHO-teh-ra.*

74. Slowly. Ἀργά. *ahr-GHA.*

75. Slower. Ἀργότερα. *ahr-GHO-teh-ra.*

76. Quickly. Γρήγορα. *GHREE-gho-ra.*

77. Faster. Γρηγορώτερα.
ghree-gho-RO-teh-ra.

78. Come here. Ἐλᾶτε ἐδῶ.
eh-LA-teh eh-THOH.

79. Come in. Ἐλᾶτε μέσα.
eh-LA-teh MEH-sa.

80. It is early. Εἶναι νωρίς.
EE-neh no-REESS.

81. It is (too) late. Εἶναι (πολὺ) ἀργά.
EE-neh (po-LEE) ahr-GHA.

82. Men's room. ΑΝΔΡΩΝ. *ahn-THROHN.*

83. Ladies' room. ΓΥΝΑΙΚΩΝ.
yee-neh-KOHN.

84. Where is the toilet? Ποῦ εἶναι τὸ μέρος;
POO EE-neh toh-MEH-rohss?

85. I am warm (cold).
Ζεσταίνομαι (κρυώνω).
zeh-STEH-no-meh (kree-OH-no).

86. I am hungry (thirsty, sleepy).
Πεινῶ (διψῶ, νυστάζω).
pee-NO (theep-SO, nee-STA-zo).

87. I am (not) in a hurry.
(Δὲν) βιάζομαι.
(then) vee-AH-zo-meh.

88. I am busy (tired, ill).
Εἶμαι ἀπησχολημένος (κουρασμένος, ἄρρω-
στος).
*EE-meh ah-pee-skho-lee-MEH-nohss (koo-ra-
ZMEH-nohss, AH-rohss-tohss).*

89. I am lost.
Ἔχασα τὸ δρόμο (μου).
EH-kha-sa toh-THRO-mo-(moo).

90. I am looking for ——.
Ψάχνω γιά ——.
PSA-khno ya ——.

91. I am glad.
Χαίρω.
KHEH-ro.

92. I am sorry.
Λυποῦμαι.
lee-POO-meh.

93. I am ready.
Εἶμαι ἕτοιμος.
EE-meh EH-tee-mohss.

94. Can you tell me?
Μπορεῖτε νὰ μοῦ πῆτε;
bo-REE-teh na-moo-PEE-teh?

95. What is that?
Τὶ εἶναι αὐτό;
TEE EE-neh af-TOH?

96. I should like ——.
Θὰ ἤθελα ——.
tha-EE-theh-la ——.

97. Can you recommend?
Μπορεῖτε νὰ μοῦ συστήσετε;
bo-REE-teh na-moo-see-STEE-seh-teh?

98. Do you want ——?
Θέλετε ——;
THEH-leh-teh ——?

99. I (do not) know.
(Δὲν) ξέρω.
(then) KSEH-ro.

100. I (do not) think so.
(Δὲν) νομίζω.
(then) no-MEE-zo.

DIFFICULTIES

103. I cannot find my hotel address.

Δὲν μπορῶ νὰ βρῶ τὴ διεύθυνση τοῦ ξενοδοχείου.

ᵗhen bo-RO na-VRO tee-ᵗhee-EF-theen-see too kseh-no-ᵗho-KHEE-oo.

104. I do not remember the street.

Δὲν θυμοῦμαι τὸ δρόμο.

ᵗhen thee-MOO-meh to-THRO-moh.

105. I have lost my friends.

Ἔχασα τοὺς φίλους μου.

EH-kha-sa toos FEE-looz-moo.

106. I left my purse (or wallet) in the ——.

Ἄφησα τὸ πορτοφόλι μου στό ——.

AH-fee-sa toh-po-rto-FO-lee-moo sto ——.

107. I forgot my money (keys).

Λησμόνησα τὰ λεφτά μου (κλειδιά μου).

lee-ZMO-nee-sa ta-leh-FTA-moo (klee-THYA moo).

108. I have missed my train (plane, bus).

Ἔχασα τὸ τραῖνο (ἀεροπλάνο, λεωφορεῖο).

EH-kha-sa toh TREH-no (ah-eh-ro-PLA-no, leh-oh-fo-REE-o).

109. What is the matter here?

Τὶ συμβαίνει ἐδῶ;

TEE seem-VEH-nee eh-THOH?

110. What am I to do?

Τὶ πρέπει νὰ κάνω;

TEE PREH-pee na-KA-no?

111. It is (not) my fault.

(Δὲν) εἶναι δικό μου λάθος.

(*then*) *EE-neh* ‾*thee-KO-moo LA-thohss.*

112. They are bothering me.

Μ'ἐνοχλοῦν.

meh-no-KHLOON.

113. Go away.

Φύγετε.

FEE-yeh-teh.

114. Where is the American consul?

Ποῦ εἶναι ὁ ἀμερικανὸς πρόξενος;

POO EE-neh o ah-meh-ree-ka-NOHSS PRO-kseh-nohss?

115. I will call a policeman.

Θὰ   φωνάξω   ἕναν   ἀστυφύλακα (or
ἕνα χωροφύλακα).

*tha fo-NA-kso EH-nahn ass-tee-FEE-la-ka (or
EH-na kho-ro-FEE-la-ka).*

In Athens the policeman is called ἀστυφύλακας, but in the
other cities and towns he is called χωροφύλακας.

116. Where is the police station?

Ποῦ εἶναι ὁ ἀστυνομικὸς σταθμός;

*POO EE-neh o ass-tee-no-mee-KOHSS sta-
THMOHSS?*

117. I have been robbed of ——.

Μ'ἔκλεψαν ——.

MEH-kleh-psahn ——.

118. The lost and found desk.

Γραφεῖον ἀπολεσθέντων καὶ εὑρεθέντων.

*ghra-FEE-ohn ah-po-less-THEN-dohn keh eh-
vreh-THEN-dohn.*

119. Help! Fire! Thief!
Βοήθεια! Φωτιά! Κλέφτης!
vo-EE-thee-ah! fo-TYA! or *fo-tee-AH!*
KLEF-teess!

120. Look (out)! Stop! Listen!
Προσέξτε! Σταματῆστε! Ἀκοῦστε!
pro-SEX-teh! sta-ma-TEE-steh!
ah-KOO-steh!

GREETINGS AND INTRODUCTIONS

123. Good morning (Good day).   Good afternoon or Good evening.
Καλημέρα. Καλησπέρα.
ka-lee-MEH-ra. ka-lee-SPEH-ra.

124. Hello. Good-bye.
Γειά σας. Χαίρετε (or Ἀντίο).
YA-sass. KHEH-reh-teh (or ah(n)-DEE-o).

125. I'll see you. Good night.
Θὰ σᾶς δῶ. Καληνύκτα.
tha-sahz-$\overline{THO}$. ka-lee-NEEKH-ta.

126. What is your name?
Πῶς ὀνομάζεσθε (or πῶς σᾶς λένε);
POHSS o-no-MAH-zess-theh (or POHSS saz-LEH-neh)?

127. May I introduce Mr. (Mrs., Miss) ——?
Μπορῶ νὰ σᾶς συστήσω τὸν κύριο (τὴν κυρία, τὴ δεσποινίδα) ——;
bo-RO na-sass-see-STEE-so tohn-GEE-ree-o (teen-gee-REE-a, tee-$\overline{thess}$-pee-NEE-$\overline{tha}$)—?

128. My wife.   My husband.
'Η γυναίκα μου. 'Ο ἄντρας μου.
ee yee-NEH-ka-moo.   o AHN-draz-moo.

129. My daughter.   My son.
'Η θυγατέρα μου (or ἡ κόρη μου).'Ο γιός μου.
ee thee-gha-TEH-ra-moo (or ee KO-ree-moo).
o YOZ-moo.

130. My friend.   My relative.
'Ο φίλος μου *m.*,   ἡ φίλη μου *f.*
'Ο συγγενής μου.
o FEE-loz-moo, ee FEE-lee-moo.   o seen-geh-
NEEZ-moo.

131. My sister.   My brother.
'Η ἀδελφή μου.   'Ο ἀδελφός μου.
ee ah-thel-FEE-moo.   o ah-thel-FOHZ-moo.

132. I am a friend of Mr. ——.
Εἶμαι φίλος τοῦ κυρίου ——.
EE-meh FEE-loss too kee-REE-oo ——.

133. I am happy to make your acquaintance.
Χαίρω πολύ.
KHEH-ro po-LEE.

134. How are you?
Πῶς εἶσθε;
POHSS EESS-theh?

135. Fine, thanks.   And you?
Καλά, εὐχαριστῶ. Καὶ σεῖς;
ka-LA, ef-kha-ree-STO. keh SEESS?

136. How is your family?

Πῶς εἶναι ἡ οἰκογένειά σας;

POHSS EE-neh ee ee-ko-GHE-nee-AH-sass?

137. (Not) very well.

("Όχι) πολὺ καλά.

(O-khee) po-LEE ka-LA.

138. Sit down, please.

Καθῆστε, παρακαλῶ.

ka-THEE-steh, pa-ra-ka-LO.

139. I have enjoyed myself very much.

Εὐχαριστήθηκα παρὰ πολύ.

ef-kha-ree-STEE-thee-ka pa-ra-po-LEE.

140. I hope to see you again soon.

'Ελπίζω νὰ σᾶς ξαναϊδῶ σύντομα.

el-PEE-zo na-sass-ksa-na-ee-$\overline{THO}$ SEEN-do-ma.

141. Come to see me (us).

'Ελᾶτε νὰ μὲ (μᾶς) δῆτε.

eh-LA-teh na meh (mass) $\overline{THEE}$-teh.

142. Give me your address (and telephone number).

Δῶστέ μου τὴ διεύθυνσή σας (καὶ τὸν ἀριθμὸ τοῦ τηλεφώνου σας).

$\overline{THO}$-steh-moo tee thee-EF-theen-SEE-sass (keh tohn-ah-ree-THMO too tee-le-FO-noo-sass).

143. Give my regards to ——.

(Δῶστε) τοὺς χαιρετισμούς μου στὸ *m.* στὴ *f.* ——.

($\overline{THO}$-steh) toos khe-re-teez-MOOZ-moo sto, stee ——.

144. We are travelling to Athens.
Ταξιδεύομε γιὰ τὴν 'Αθήνα.
ta-ksee-THEV-o-meh ya teen ah-THEE-na.

145. Congratulations.
Συγχαρητήρια.
seegh-kha-ree-TEE-ree-ah.

146. Happy Birthday or **Happy Nameday.**
Χρόνια πολλά. (lit. Many Years)
KHRO-nya po-LA.

147. Merry Christmas.
Καλὰ Χριστούγεννα.
ka-LA khree-STOO-yeh-nah.

148. Happy New Year.
Εὐτυχὲς τὸ νέον ἔτος.
ef-tee-KHESS toh NEH-ohn EH-tohss.

149. May I have a date with you for (next) Wednesday?
Μπορῶ νὰ ἔχω ραντεβοῦ μαζί σας τὴν (ἐρχόμενη) Τετάρτη;
bo-RO na E-kho rahn-de-VOO ma-ZEE-sahss teen (er-KHO-me-nee) teh-TAR-tee?

TRAVEL: GENERAL EXPRESSIONS

150. Can you direct me to a travel agency?
Μπορεῖτε νὰ μὲ ὁδηγήσετε σ' ἕνα ταξιδιωτικὸ πρακτορεῖο;
bo-REE-teh na meh oh-thee-GHEE-seh-teh SEH-na ta-ksee-thee-o-tee-KO pra-kto-REE-o?

151. I want to go to the airport (bus station).

Θέλω νὰ πάω στὸ ἀεροδρόμιο (στὴ στάση τῶν λεωφορείων).

THEH-lo na PA-o sto ah-eh-ro-$\overline{THRO}$-mee-o (stee STA-see tohn leh-o-fo-REE-ohn).

152. Is the railroad station near here?

Εἶναι ὁ σιδηροδρομικὸς σταθμὸς πλησίον;

EE-neh o see-$\overline{thee}$-ro-$\overline{thro}$-mee-KOHSS sta-THMOHSS plee-SEE-ohn?

153. What is the best way of travelling?

Ποιὸς εἶναι ὁ καλύτερος τρόπος νὰ ταξιδεύσω;

pee-OHSS EE-neh o ka-LEE-teh-rohss TRO-pohss na tah-ksee-$\overline{THEF}$-so?

154. How long will it take to go to —— ?

Πωσο θὰ μέ πάρη νὰ πάω στὸ (or στὴ *f.*) ——;

PO-so tha meh PAH-ree nah PA-o sto (or stee) ——?

155. When will we arrive at —— ?

Πότε θὰ φθάσωμε στὸ (or στὴ *f.*) ——;

PO-teh tha FTHA-so-meh sto (or stee) ——?

156. Please call me a taxi.

Σᾶς παρακαλῶ φωνάξτε ἕνα αὐτοκίνητο.

sass pa-ra-kaLO foh-NAXT-eh EH-na ahf-toh-KEE-nee-toh.

157. Where is the baggage room?

Ποῦ εἶναι ὁ θάλαμος ἀποσκευῶν;

POO EE-neh o THA-la-mohss ah-po-skev-OHN?

158. I need a porter.

Θέλω ἕναν ἀχθοφόρο.

THEH-lo EH-nahn ah-khtho-FO-ro.

159. Follow me, please.

'Ακολουθῆστέ με παρακαλῶ.

ah-ko-loo-THEE-steh-meh pa-ra-ka-LO.

160. Can I reserve a (front) seat?

Μπορῶ νὰ κρατήσω μία θέση (ἐμπρός);

bo-RO no kra-TEE-so MEE-ah THEH-see (em-BROHSS)?

161. I want a seat near the window.

Θέλω μία θέση κοντὰ στὸ παράθυρο.

THEH-lo MEE-ah THEH-see ko-DA sto pa-RA-thee-ro.

162. Is this seat taken?

Εἶναι αὐτὴ ἡ θέση πιασμένη;

EE-neh ahf-TEE ee THEH-see pya-ZMEH-nee?

163. Where is the nearest station?

Ποῦ εἶναι ὁ πλησιέστερος σταθμός;

POO EE-neh o plee-see-ESS-teh-rohss sta-THMOHSS?

164. Is this the (direct) way to ——?

Εἶναι αὐτὸς ὁ δρόμος (ποὺ πηγαίνει κατ' εὐθεῖαν) γιά ——;

EE-neh ahf-TOHSS o $\overline{THRO}$-mohss (poo pee-YEN-ee ka-tef-THEE-ahn) ya ——?

165. Which is the quicker?

Ποιός εἶναι ὁ γρηγορώτερος;

PYOHSS EE-neh o ghree-gho-RO-teh-rohss?

166. How does one go (there)?
Πῶς πηγαίνει κανεὶς (ἐκεῖ);
POHSS pee-YEN-ee ka-NEESS (eh-KEE)?

167. Show me on the map.
Δεῖξτέ μου στὸ χάρτη.
THEEK-steh-moo sto KHAR-tee.

168. Does it stop at ——?
Σταματᾶ στὸ (or στή *f.*) ——;
sta-ma-TAH sto (or stee) ——?

169. Is there a subway?
Ἔχει ὑπόγειο σιδηρόδρομο;
EH-khee ee-PO-yee-o see-thee-RO-thro-mo?

170. Where do I turn?
Ποῦ νὰ στρίψω;
POO na STREEP-so?

171. To the north. Βόρεια. *VOR-ee-ah.*

172. To the south. Νότια. *NOHT-ee-ah.*

173. To the east. Ἀνατολικά. *ah-na-to-lee-KAH.*

174. To the west. Δυτικά. *thee-tee-KAH.*

175. To the right. Δεξιά. *theks-ee-AH.*

176. To the left. Ἀριστερά. *ah-ree-steh-RA.*

177. Straight ahead. Κατ' εὐθεῖαν ἐμπρός.
ka-tef-THEE-ahn em-BROHSS.

178. Corner. Γωνία. *gho-NEE-ah.*

179. Forward. Ἐμπρός. *em-BROHSS.*

180. Back. Πίσω. *PEE-so.*

181. Street. Δρόμος or Οδός.
$\overline{THRO}$-mohss or oh-$\overline{THOHSS}$.

182. Avenue or **boulevard.** Λεωφόρος.
leh-o-FO-rohss.

183. Square. Πλατεῖα. pla-TEE-ah.

184. Park. Πάρκο. PAR-ko.

185. Am I going in the right direction?
Ἔχω τή σωστή κατεύθυνση;
EH-kho tee so-STEE ka-TEF-theen-see?

186. Please show me.
Παρακαλῶ δεῖξτέ μου.
pah-ra-ka-LO $\overline{THEEK}$-steh-moo.

187. What street is this?
Ποιός δρόμος εἶναι αὐτός;
PYOHSS $\overline{THRO}$-mohss EE-neh ahf-TOHSS?

188. Do I have to change?
Πρέπει ν' ἀλλάξω;
PREH-pee na-LA-kso?

189. Please tell me where to get off.
Παρακαλῶ πέστε μου ποῦ νά βγῶ.
pa-ra-ka-LO PEH-steh-moo POO na VGHO.

AT THE CUSTOMS

192. Where is the customs?
Ποῦ εἶναι τό τελωνεῖο;
POO EE-neh toh teh-lo-NEE-o?

193. Here is my baggage, —— pieces.

Ἐδῶ εἶναι τὰ πράγματά μου, —— τεμάχια.

eh-THO EE-neh tah PRAGH-mah-tah-moo,
—— *teh-MAH-khee-ah.*

194. This package contains clothing (food, books).

Αὐτὸ τὸ δέμα (περι)έχει ροῦχα (τρόφιμα, βιβλία).

ahf-TOH toh THEH-ma (peh-ree)-EH-khee ROO-kha (TRO-fee-ma, vee-VLEE-a).

195. Here is my passport (visa).

Ὁρίστε τὸ διαβατήριό μου (ἡ βίζα μου).

oh-REE-steh toh thee-ah-va-TEE-ree-O-moo (ee VEE-zah-moo).

196. I have my landing ticket (permit).

Ἔχω εἰσιτήριο (ἄδεια) ἀποβιβάσεως.

EH-kho ee-see-TEE-ree-o (AH-thee-a) ah-po-vee-VA-seh-ohss.

197. I am a tourist.

Εἶμαι τουριστής.

EE-meh too-reess-TEESS.

198. This is a business visit.

Αὐτὴ εἶναι ἐμπορικὴ ἐπίσκεψη.

ahf-TEE EE-neh em-bo-ree-KEE eh-PEE-skep-see.

199. I am in transit.

Εἶμαι περαστικός.

EE-meh peh-rass-tee-KOHSS.

200. Must I open everything?

Πρέπει νὰ τ' ἀνοίξω ὅλα;

PREH-pee nah-ta-NEE-kso OH-la?

201. I cannot open that.

Δὲν μπορῶ νὰ τὸ ἀνοίξω αὐτό.

then bo-RO na-toh-ah-NEE-kso ahf-TOH.

202. I have nothing to declare.

Δὲν ἔχω τίποτε νὰ δηλώσω.

then EH-kho TEE-po-teh na-thee-LO-so.

203. All this is for my personal use.

Ὅλα αὐτὰ εἶναι γιὰ προσωπικὴ μου
χρήση.

*OH-la ahf-TAH EE-neh ya pro-so-pee-KEE-
moo KHREE-see.*

204. There is nothing here but ——.

Δὲν ἔχει τίποτε ἐδῶ ἐκτὸς ἀπὸ ——.

*then EH-khee TEE-po-te eh-THO ek-TOHSS
ah-PO ——.*

205. These are gifts.

Αὐτὰ εἶναι δῶρα.

ahf-TA EE-neh THO-ra.

206. Are these things dutiable?

Εἶναι αὐτὰ τὰ πράγματα φορολογήσιμα;

*EE-neh ahf-TA ta PRAGH-ma-ta fo-ro-lo-
GHEE-see-ma?*

207. How much must I pay?

Πόσο πρέπει νὰ πληρώσω;

PO-so PREH-pee na plee-RO-so?

208. This is all I have.

Αὐτά εἶναι ὅλα ποὺ ἔχω.

ahf-TA EE-neh OH-la poo EH-kho.

209. Please be careful.

Παρακαλῶ προσέξτε.

pah-ra-ka-LO pro-SEK-steh.

210. Have you finished?

Τελειώσατε;

te-lee-OH-sa-teh?

211. I cannot find all my baggage.

Δὲν μπορῶ νὰ βρῶ ὅλα τὰ πράγματά μου.

then bo-RO na-VRO OH-la tah PRAGH-ma-ta-moo.

212. My train leaves in —— minutes.

Τὸ τραῖνό μου φεύγει σὲ —— λεπτά.

toh TREH-no-moo FEV-yee seh —— lep-TA.

TICKETS

215. Where is the ticket office?

Ποῦ εἶναι ἡ θυρίδα τῶν εἰσιτηρίων;

POO EE-neh ee thee-REE-tha tohn ee-see-tee-REE-ohn?

216. I need a ticket to ——. A timetable.

Θέλω ἕνα εἰσιτήριο γιὰ ——. Δρομολόγιο.

THE-lo EH-na ee-see-TEE-ree-o ya ——. thro-mo-LO-yee-o.

217. How much is a one-way (round trip) ticket to ——?

Πόσο ἔχει ἕνα εἰσιτήριο (μετ' ἐπιστροφῆς) γιά —;

PO-so EH-khee EH-nah ee-see-TEE-ree-o (meh-teh-pee-stro-FEESS) ya ——?

218. First (second, third) class.

Πρώτη (δευτέρα, τρίτη) θέσις.

PRO-tee (thef-TEH-ra, TREE-tee) THEH-seess.

219. Is there an express train to ——?

Ἔχει ἐξπρὲς τραῖνο γιά —;

EH-khee eks-PRESS TREH-no ya ——?

220. A reserved seat.

Κρατημένη θέση.

kra-tee-MEH-nee THEH-see.

221. Can I go by way of ——?

Μπορῶ νὰ πάω ἀπὸ —;

bo-RO na PA-o ah-PO ——?

222. Is there a later (earlier) train?

Ἔχει τραῖνο πιὸ ἀργὰ (νωρίς);

EH-khee TREH-no pyo ahr-GHA (no-REESS)?

223. From what station (track) do I leave?

'Απὸ ποιὸ σταθμὸ (ποιά γραμμὴ) θὰ φύγω;

ah-po PYO stah-THMO (PYAH ghra-MEE) tha FEE-gho?

224. How long is this ticket good?

Γιὰ πόσον καιρὸ ἰσχύει αὐτὸ τὸ εἰσιτήριο;
ya PO-son geh-RO ee-SKHEE-ee af-TOH toh ee-see-TEE-ree-o?

225. Can I get something to eat on the way?

Μπορῶ νὰ βρῶ τίποτε νὰ φάω στὸ δρόμο;
bo-RO na VRO TEE-po-teh na FA-o sto $\overline{THRO}$-*mo?*

226. How much baggage may I take?

Πόσα πράγματα μπορῶ νὰ πάρω;
PO-sa PRAGH-ma-ta bo-RO na-PA-ro?

BAGGAGE

230. Where is the baggage checked?

Ποῦ ἐλέγχονται οἱ ἀποσκευές;
POO eh-LEGH-khon-deh ee ah-po-skev-ESS?

231. I want to leave these bags for a while.

Θέλω νὰ ἀφήσω αὐτὲς τὶς βαλίτσες γιὰ λίγο.
THEH-lo na ah-FEE-so ahf-TESS teez vah-LEE-tsess ya LEE-gho.

232. Do I pay now or later?

Θὰ πληρώσω τώρα ἢ ἀργότερα;
tha plee-RO-so TOR-ah ee ahr-GHO-teh-ra?

233. I want to take out my baggage.

Θέλω νὰ πάρω τὰ πράγματά μου.
THEH-lo na-PA-ro tu PRAGH-ma-TA-moo.

234. Those things over there are mine.

Αὐτὰ ἐκεῖ εἶναι δικά μου.

ahf-TAH eh-KEE EE-neh ͞thee-KA-moo.

235. Handle this very carefully.

Πιάστε το πολὺ προσεκτικά.

PYA-steh-toh po-LEE pro-seh-ktee-KA.

236. Where can I find the stationmaster?

Ποῦ μπορῶ νὰ βρῶ τὸ σταθμάρχη;

POO bo-RO na-VRO toh-sta-THMAR-khee?

AIRPLANE

239. Is there bus service to the airport?

Ἔχει λεωφορεῖο γιὰ τὸ ἀεροδρόμιο;

EH-khee leh-o-fo-REE-o ya toh a-e-ro-͞THRO-mee-o?

240. At what time will they come for me?

Τὶ ὥρα θὰ ἔλθουν γιὰ μένα;

TEE OR-ah tha-EL-thoon ya MEH-na?

241. When is there a plane to —— ?

Πότε ἔχει ἀεροπλάνο γιὰ —;

PO-teh EH-khee a-e-ro-PLA-no ya ——?

242. What is the flight number?

Ποῖος εἶναι ὁ ἀριθμὸς πτήσεως;

PEE-ohss EE-neh o ah-ree-THMOHSS PTEE-seh-ohss?

243. Is food served on the plane?

Σερβίρονται τρόφιμα στὸ ἀεροπλάνο;

ser-VEE-ron-deh TRO-fee-ma sto a-e-ro-PLA-no?

244. How many kilograms may I take?

Πόσα κιλὰ μπορῶ νὰ πάρω;

PO-sa kee-LA bo-RO na-PA-ro?

245. How much is it per kilogram for excess?

Πόσο ἔχει τὸ κιλὸ γιὰ ὅτι εἶναι παραπάνω;

PO-so EH-khee toh-kee-LO ya OH-tee EE-neh par-ra-PA-no?

246. Fasten your safety belts please.

Σφίξτε τὶς ζῶνες ἀσφαλείας παρακαλῶ.

SFEEK-steh teess ZO-ness ass-fah-LEE-ass pa-ra-ka-LO.

BOAT

248. Can I go by boat to ——?

Μπορῶ νὰ πάω μὲ πλοῖο στὸ (στή *f.*) ——;

bo-RO na-PAH-o meh PLEE-o sto (or stee) ——?

249. When does the next boat leave?

Πότε φεύγει τὸ ἐπόμενο πλοῖο;

PO-teh FEV-yee toh eh-PO-meh-no PLEE-o?

250. When must I go on board?

Πότε πρέπει νὰ ἀνεβῶ στὸ πλοῖο;

PO-teh PREH-pee nah-ah-nev-O sto PLEE-o?

251. Can I land at ——?

Μπορῶ νά ἀποβιβασθῶ στὸ (or στή *f.*)——;

bo-RO nah-a-po-vee-vass-THO sto (or stee) ——?

252. The captain.   The officer.

Ὁ πλοίαρχος.   Ὁ ἀξιωματικός.

o   PLEE-ar-khohss.   o   ah-ksee-oh-ma-tee-KOHSS.

253. The deck.   Upper.   Lower.

Τὸ κατάστρωμα.   Ἐπάνω.   Κάτω.

toh-ka-TA-stro-ma.   eh-PA-no.   KA-toh.

254. Where can I find the purser (steward)?

Ποῦ μπορῶ νὰ βρῶ τὸν ταμία (στιούαρτ) τοῦ πλοίου;

POO   bo-RO   na-VRO   tohn-da-MEE-a (STEW-art) too-PLEE-oo?

255. I want to rent a deck chair.

Θέλω νὰ ἐνοικιάσω ἕνα κάθισμα στὸ κατάστρωμα.

THEH-lo   nah-eh-nee-kee-AH-so   EH-na   KA-theez-ma sto ka-TASS-tro-ma.

256. I am seasick.

Μ' ἐζάλισε ἡ θάλασσα.

meh-ZA-lee-seh ee THA-lass-ah.

257. Please prepare my berth.

Παρακαλῶ ἑτοιμάστε τὸ κρεβάτι μου.

pah-ra-ka-LO   eh-tee-MASS-teh   toh   kreh-VAH-tee-moo.

258. I am going to my stateroom.

Πηγαίνω στὴν καμπίνα μου.

pee-YEN-o steen-ga-BEE-na-moo.

259. Will you close the porthole?

Παρακαλῶ κλεῖστε τὸ παραθυράκι.

pah-ra-ka-LO KLEE-steh toh pa-ra-thee-RA-kee.

260. Let's go to the dining room.

Πᾶμε στὸ ἑστιατόριο.

PA-meh sto ess-tee-ah-TOH-ree-o.

261. Can I have breakfast in my cabin?

Μπορῶ νὰ ἔχω πρόγευμα στὴν καμπίνα μου;

bo-RO na EH-kho PRO-yev-ma steen-ga-BEE-na-moo?

262. A life boat. A life preserver.

Ναυαγοσωστικὴ βάρκα. Σωσίβιο.

nah-vah-gho-so-stee-KEE VAR-ka. so-SEE-vee-o.

BUS

265. Where is the bus station?

Ποῦ εἶναι ἡ στάση τῶν λεωφορείων;

POO EE-neh ee STA-see tohn leh-oh-fo-REE-ohn?

266. Can I buy an excursion ticket?

Μπορῶ ν' ἀγοράσω ἕνα εἰσιτήριο ἔκδρομῆς;

bo-RO na-gho-RA-so EH-na ee-see-TEE-ree-o ehk-throh-MEESS?

267. Is there a stop for lunch?

Θὰ σταματήση γιὰ νὰ φᾶμε;

tha sta-ma-TEE-see ya na-FA-meh?

268. May I stop on the way?

Μπορῶ νὰ σταματήσω στὸ δρόμο;

bo-RO na-sta-ma-TEE-so sto THRO-mo?

AUTOMOBILE

271. Where is a gas station (garage)?

Ποῦ εἶναι τὸ γκαράζ;

POO EE-neh to-ga-RAHZ?

272. Is the road good (paved)?

Εἶναι ὁ δρόμος καλὸς (ἀσφαλτοστρωμένος);

EE-neh o THRO-mohss ka-LOSS (ass-fal-toh-stro-MEH-nohss)?

273. What town is this (the next one)?

Ποιὸ χωριὸ εἶναι αὐτὸ (τὸ ἑπόμενο);

PYO kho-RYO EE-neh ahf-TOH (toh eh-PO-meh-no)?

274. Where does that road go?

Ποῦ πηγαίνει αὐτὸς ὁ δρόμος;

POO pee-YEN-ee ahf-TOHSS o THRO-mohss?

275. Can you show it to me on the map?

Μπορεῖτε νὰ μοῦ τὸ δείξτε στὸ χάρτη;

bo-REE-teh na moo toh THEEK-steh sto KHAR-tee?

276. The tourist club.

Περιηγητική Λέσχη.

per-ee-ee-ghee-tee-KEE LESS-khee.

277. I have an (international) driver's licence.

Ἔχω (διεθνῆ) ἄδεια ὁδηγοῦ.

EH-kho (thee-eth-NEE) AH-thee-a oh-thee-GHOO.

278. How much is gas a gallon?

Πόσο ἔχει ἕνα γαλόνι βενζίνη;

PO-so EH-khee EH-na gha-LO-nee ven-ZEE-nee?

279. Give me —— liters.

Δῶστε μου —— λίτρες.

THO-steh-moo —— LEE-tress.

280. Please change the oil.

Παρακαλῶ ἀλλάξτε τὸ λάδι.

pa-ra-ka-LO ah-LAK-steh toh LAH-thee.

281. Light (medium, heavy) oil.

Ἐλαφρὸ (μέτριο, βαρὺ) μηχανέλαιο.

eh-laff-RO (MET-ree-o, va-REE) mee-kha-NEH-leh-o.

282. Put water in the battery.

Βάλτε νερὸ στὴ μπαταρία.

VAL-teh neh-RO stee ba-ta-REE-a.

283. Recharge the battery.

Ξαναγεμίστε τὴ μπαταρία.

ksa-na-yeh-MEE-steh tee ba-ta-REE-a.

34 **AUTOMOBILE**

284. Will you lubricate the car?

Παρακαλῶ λαδῶστε τὸ αὐτοκίνητο.

pah-ra-ka-LO la-$\overline{THO}$-steh toh ahf-toh-KEE-nee-toh.

285. Could you wash it now (soon)?

Θὰ μπορούσατε νὰ τὸ πλύνετε τώρα (σύντομα);

tha bo-ROO-sah-teh na toh PLEE-neh-teh TOR-ah (SEEN-do-ma)?

286. Tighten the brakes.

Σφίξτε τὰ φρένα.

SFEEK-steh ta FREH-na.

287. Will you check the tires?

Παρακαλῶ κοιτάξτε τὰ λάστιχα.

pah-ra-ka-LO kee-TAHK-steh ta LASS-tee-kha.

288. Can you fix the flat tire?

Μπορεῖτε νὰ διορθῶστε τὸ σπασμένο λάστιχο;

bo-REE-teh na $\overline{thee}$-or-THOHSS-teh toh spaz-MEH-no LASS-tee-kho?

289. Can you recommend a good mechanic?

Μπορεῖτε νὰ μοῦ συστήσετε ἕναν καλὸ μηχανικό;

bo-REE-teh na moo see-STEE-seh-teh EH-nahn-ga-LO mee-kha-nee-KO?

290. I want some air.

Θέλω λίγο ἀέρα.

THEH-lo LEE-gho ah-EH-ra.

291. A puncture.   A slow leak.
Σπάσιμο. Σιγοτρέχει.
SPAH-see-mo.   see-gho-TREH-khee.

292. The horn does not work well.
Τὸ κλάξον δὲν δουλεύει καλά.
to KLA-ksohn then thoo-LEV-ee ka-LA.

293. Can you give me a lift to the village?
Μπορεῖτε νὰ μὲ πᾶτε στὸ χωριό;
bo-REE-teh na meh PA-teh sto kho-RYO?

294. What is wrong?
Τί ἔχει;
TEE EH-khee?

295. There is a grinding (leak, noise).
Τρίζει (τρέχει, κάνει θόρυβο).
*TREE-zee (TREH-khee, KAH-nee THO-
ree-vo).*

296. The engine overheats.
Ἡ μηχανὴ ζεσταίνεται πολύ.
ee mee-kha-NEE zest-EH-neh-teh po-LEE.

297. The engine misses (stalls).
Ἡ μηχανὴ χάνει (σταματᾶ).
ee mee-kha-NEE KHA-nee (sta-ma-TA).

298. There is a rattle (squeak).
Γιγλίζει (τρίζει).
ghee-GLEE-zee (TREE-zee).

299. May I park here for a while?
Μπορῶ νὰ σταθμεύσω ἐδῶ γιὰ λίγο;
*bo-RO na-sta-THMEF-so eh-THO ya LEE-
gho?*

300. I want to garage my car for the night.

Θέλω νὰ βάλω τὸ αὐτοκίνητό μου στὸ γκαράζ γι' ἀπόψε.

THEH-lo na-VAH-lo toh ahf-toh-KEE-nee-toh-moo sto-ga-RAZ ya-POH-pseh.

301. When does it open (close)?

Πότε ἀνοίγει (κλείνει);

PO-teh ah-NEE-ghee (KLEE-nee)?

PARTS OF THE CAR

304. Accelerator. Γκάζ. *GAHZ.*

305. Battery. Μπαταρία. *ba-ta-REE-ah.*

306. Bolt. Μπουλόνι. *boo-LO-nee.*

307. Brake. Φρένο. *FREH-no.*

308. Engine. Μηχανή. *mee-kha-NEE.*

309. Headlight. Μπροστινὸ φῶς. *bro-stee-NO FOHSS.*

310. Horn. Κλάξον. *KLA-ksohn.*

311. Motor. Μοτέρ. *moTER.*

312. Nut. Παξιμάδι. *pa-ksee-MA-thee.*

313. Spring. 'Ελατήριο. *eh-la-TEE-ree-o.*

314. Starter. Μίζα. *MEE-za.*

315. Steering wheel. Τιμόνι. *tee-MO-nee.*

316. Tail light. Πίσω φῶς. *PEE-so FOHSS.*

317. Tire. Λάστιχο. *LASS-tee-kho.*

318. Spare tire. Ἔξτρα λάστιχο. *EX-tra LASS-tee-kho.*

319. Wheel. Ρόδα. *RO-thah.*

320. Windshield wiper. Καθαριστήρι τῶν τζαμιῶν. *ka-tha-ree-STEE-ree tohn tza-MYOHN.*

TOOLS AND EQUIPMENT

323. Chains. Άλυσίδες. *al-ee-SEE-thess.*

324. Hammer. Σφυρί. *sfee-REE.*

325. Jack. Γρύλος. *GHREE-loss.*

326. Key. Κλειδί. *klee-THEE.*

327. Pliers. Ντανάλια. *da-NA-lyah.*

328. Rope. Σχοινί. *skhee-NEE.*

329. Screwdriver. Βιδολόγος. *vee-tho-LO-ghohss.*

330. Tire pump. Τρούμπα or ἀεραντλία.
TROOM-bah or ah-er-and-LEE-ah.

331. Wrench. Γαλλικὸ κλειδί. *gha-lee-KO klee-THEE.*

HELP ON THE ROAD

334. I am sorry to trouble you.
Μὲ συγχωρεῖτε ποὺ σᾶς ἐνοχλῶ.
meh seegh-kho-REE-teh poo sass eh-no-KHLO.

335. My car has broken down.
Τὸ αὐτοκίνητό μου χάλασε.
toh ahf-toh-KEE-nee-toh-moo KHA-la-seh.

336. Can you tow (push) my car?
Μπορεῖτε νὰ ρυμολκήσετε (σπρώξετε) τὸ
αὐτοκίνητό μου;
*bo-REE-teh nah ree-mol-KEE-seh-teh (SPRO-
kseh-teh) toh ahf-toh-KEE-nee-TOH-moo?*

337. Can you give me a lift to ——?
Μπορεῖτε νὰ μὲ πᾶτε στὸ (or στή *f.*) ——;
bo-REE-teh nah meh PA-teh sto (or stee) ——?

338. Can you help me jack up the car?

Μπορεῖτε νὰ μὲ βοηθῆστε νὰ σηκώσω τὸ
αὐτοκίνητό μου;

*bo-REE-teh na meh voh-ee-THEE-steh na
see-KO-so toh ahf-toh-KEE-nee-toh-moo?*

339. Will you help me put on the spare?

Μπορεῖτε νὰ μὲ βοηθῆστε ν' ἀλλάξω τὸ
λάστιχο;

*bo-REE-teh na me vo-ee-THEE-steh na-LA-
kso toh LASS-tee-kho?*

340. Could you give me some gas?

Μπορεῖτε νὰ μοῦ δῶστε λίγη βενζίνη;

*bo-REE-teh na moo $\overline{THO}$-steh LEE-yee ven-
ZEE-nee?*

341. Will you take me to a garage?

Μοῦ δείχνετε ἕνα γκαράζ;

moo $\overline{THEEKH}$-neh-teh EH-na ga-RAZ?

**342. Will you help me get the car off the
road?**

Θὰ μὲ βοηθήσητε νὰ βγάλω τὸ αὐτοκίνητο
ἀπὸ τὸ δρόμο;

*tha meh vo-ee-THEE-seh-teh nah-VGHA-lo
toh ahf-toh-KEE-nee-toh ah-po toh $\overline{THRO}$-mo?*

343. My car is stuck in the mud.

Τὸ αὐτοκίνητό μου ἔπεσε στῆ λάσπη.

*toh ahf-toh-KEE-nee-toh-moo EH-peh-seh stee
LASS-pee.*

344. It is in the ditch.

Εἶναι στὸ λάκκο.

EE-neh sto LA-ko.

ROAD SIGNS AND PUBLIC NOTICES

(alphabetized according to Greek)

347. Dead end. ΑΔΙΕΞΟΔΟΣ. *ah-thee-EH-kso-thohss.*
No passing or **No thoroughfare.**
ΑΠΑΓΟΡΕΥΕΤΑΙ Η ΔΙΑΒΑΣΙΣ.
ah-pah-gho-REV-eh-teh ee thee-AH-vass-eess.

348. Keep out. ΑΠΑΓΟΡΕΥΕΤΑΙ Η ΕΙΣΟΔΟΣ.
ah-pah-gho-REV-eh-teh ee EE-so-thohss.

349. No smoking. ΑΠΑΓΟΡΕΥΕΤΑΙ ΤΟ ΚΑΠΝΙΣΜΑ.
ah-pah-gho-REV-eh-teh toh KA-pneez-ma.

350. No parking. ΑΠΑΓΟΡΕΥΕΤΑΙ Η ΣΤΑΘΜΕΥΣΙΣ.
ah-pah-gho-REV-eh-teh ee STATH-mev-seess.

351. Steep grade. ΑΠΟΚΡΗΜΝΟΣ ΚΛΙΣΙΣ.
ah-PO-kree-mnohss KLEE-seess.

352. Sharp turn. ΑΠΟΤΟΜΟΣ ΣΤΡΟΦΗ.
ah-PO-toh-mohss stro-FEE.

353. Slow. ΑΡΓΑ. *ahr-GHA.*

354. High tension lines.
ΚΑΛΩΔΙΑ ΥΨΗΛΗΣ ΕΝΤΑΣΕΩΣ.
ka-LO-thee-ah eep-see-LEESS en-DA-seh-ohss.

355. Keep right. ΔΕΞΙΑ. *thek-see-AH.*

356. Intersection or **Crossroads.** ΔΙΑΣΤΑΥΡΩΣΙΣ.
thee-ass-TAV-ro-seess.

357. Double curve. ΔΙΠΛΗ ΚΑΜΠΗ.
thee-PLEE kahm-BEE.

358. Entrance. ΕΙΣΟΔΟΣ. *EE-so-thohss.*

359. Slow down. ΕΛΑΤΤΩΣΑΤΕ ΤΗΝ ΤΑΧΥΤΗΤΑ.
eh-la-TOH-sah-teh teen-da-KHEE-tee-tah.

360. Winding road. ΕΛΙΓΜΟΣ. *eh-leegh-MOHSS.*

361. Exit. ΕΞΟΔΟΣ. *EH-kso-thohss.*

362. Parking. ΕΠΙΤΡΕΠΕΤΑΙ Η ΣΤΑΘΜΕΥΣΙΣ.
eh-pee-TREH-peh-teh ee STATH-mef-seess.

363. Curve. ΚΑΜΠΗ. *kahm-BEE.*

364. Danger. ΚΙΝΔΥΝΟΣ. *KEEN-thee-nohss.*

365. Closed. ΚΛΕΙΣΤΟΝ. *klee-STOHN.*

366. Maximum speed —— kilometers per hour.
ΜΕΓΙΣΤΗ ΤΑΧΥΤΗΣ —— ΧΙΛΙΟΜΕΤΡΑ ΤΗΝ ΩΡΑ.
meh-YEE-stee ta-KHEE-teess —— khee-lee-OH-met-rah teen OR-ah.

367. No right (left) turn.
ΜΗ ΣΤΡΕΦΕΤΕ ΔΕΞΙΑ (ΑΡΙΣΤΕΡΑ).
mee STREH-feh-teh thek-see-AH (ah-ree-steh-RAH).

368. Drive carefully.
ΟΔΗΓΕΙΤΕ ΠΡΟΣΕΚΤΙΚΑ.
oh-thee-YEE-teh pro-sek-tee-KA.

369. Sound your horn.
ΠΡΟΕΙΔΟΠΟΙΗΣΑΤΕ (or Κορνάρητε).
pro-ee-tho-pee-EE-sa-teh (or kor-NAR-ee-teh).

370. Go. ΠΡΟΧΩΡΕΙΤΕ. *pro-kho-REE-teh.*

371. Railroad Crossing. ΣΙΔΗΡΟΔΡΟΜΟΣ.
see-thee-RO-thro-mohss.

372. Narrow (temporary) bridge.
ΣΤΕΝΗ (ΠΡΟΣΩΡΙΝΗ) ΓΕΦΥΡΑ.
steh-NEE (pro-so-ree-NEE) YEF-ee-ra.

373. Stop. ΣΤΑΣΙΣ. *STAH-seess.*

374. Narrow road. ΣΤΕΝΗ ΟΔΟΣ. *steh-NEE oh-THOHSS.*

375. Road repairs. ΥΠΟ ΕΠΙΔΙΟΡΘΩΣΙΝ.
ee-po eh-pee-thee-OR-tho-seen.

376. Use second gear.
ΧΡΗΣΙΜΟΠΟΙΗΣΑΤΕ ΔΕΥΤΕΡΑΝ ΤΑΧΥΤΗΤΑ.
khree-see-mo-pee-EE-sah-teh thef-TEH-rahn ta-KHEE-tee-ta.

LOCAL BUS AND STREET CAR

379. The bus stop.
Ἡ στάση τῶν λεωφορείων.
ee STAH-see tohn leh-oh-fo-REE-ohn.

380. The street car. Τὸ τράμ.
toh TRAHM.

381. The driver. Ὁ ὁδηγός.

o oh-$\overline{THEE}$-ghohss.

382. What bus (street car) do I take?

Ποιὸ λεωφορεῖο (τράμ) νὰ πάρω;

PYO leh-oh-fo-REE-o (TRAHM) na-PA-ro?

383. Where does the bus for —— stop?

Ποῦ σταματᾶ τὸ λεωφορεῖο γιὰ —— ;

POO sta-ma-TAH toh leh-oh-fo-REE-o ya ——?

384. Do you go near the palace?

Πηγαίνετε πλησίον στὰ ἀνάκτορα;

pee-YEN-et-eh plee-SEE-ohn sta ah-NA-kto-ra?

385. How much is the fare?

Πόσο ἔχει τὸ εἰσιτήριο;

PO-so EH-khee toh ee-see-TEE-ree-o?

386. I want to get off at the next stop, please.

Θέλω νὰ βγῶ στὴν ἐπομένη στάση, παρακαλῶ.

THEH-lo na-VGHO steen eh-po-MEH-nee STAH-see, pa-ra-ka-LO.

TAXI

388. Please call a taxi for me.

Παρακαλῶ φωνάξτε ἕνα αὐτοκίνητο.

pa-ra-ka-LO fo-NAHK-steh EH-nah ahf-toh-KEE-nee-toh.

389. How far is it?

Πόσο μακρυά εἶναι;

PO-so ma-kree-AH EE-neh?

390. How much will it cost?

Πόσο θὰ κοστίση;

PO-so tha ko-STEE-see?

391. That is too much.

Παρὰ πολύ.

pa-ra-po-LEE.

392. What do you charge per hour (kilometer)?

Πόσο χρειώνετε τὴν ὥρα (τὸ χιλιόμετρο);

PO-so khree-OH-neh-teh teen OR-ah (to khee-lee-O-met-ro)?

393. I wish to drive around the city.

Ἐπιθυμῶ νὰ κάνω τὸ γῦρο τῆς πόλεως.

eh-pee-thee-MO na-KA-no toh YEE-ro teess PO-leh-ohss.

394. Please drive more slowly (carefully).

Παρακαλῶ πηγαίνετε πιὸ ἀργὰ (προσεκτικά).

pa-ra-ka-LO pee-YEN-eh-teh ryo ahr-GHA (pro-sek-tee-KA).

395. Stop here.

Σταματῆστε ἐδῶ.

sta-ma-TEE-steh eh-THO.

396. Wait for me, please.

Περιμένετε, παρακαλῶ.

pe-ree-MEH-neh-teh, pah-ra-ka-LO.

397. How much do I owe you?

    Πόσο σᾶς ὀφείλω;

    PO-so sass oh-FEE-lo?

HOTEL

400. Which hotel is good (inexpensive)?

    Ποιὸ ξενοδοχεῖο εἶναι καλὸ (φθηνό);

    PYO ksen-o-tho-KHEE-o EE-neh ka-LO
    (fthee-NO)?

401. The best hotel.

    Τὸ καλύτερο ξενοδοχεῖο.

    to-ka-LEE-teh-ro ksen-o-tho-KHEE-o.

402. Not too expensive.

    Ὄχι πολὺ ἀκριβό.

    O-khee po-LEE ah-kree-VO.

403. I (do not) want to be in the center of town.

    (Δὲν) θέλω νὰ εἶμαι στὸ κέντρο τῆς πόλεως.

    (then) THEh-lo na-EE-meh sto KEN-dro
    teess PO-leh-ohss.

404. Where it is not noisy.

    Ὅπου δὲν ἔχει θόρυβο.

    O-poo then EH-khee THO-ree-vo.

405. I have a reservation for ——.

    Ἔχω ρεζερβασιὸν γιὰ ——.

    EH-kho reh-zer-va-SYOHN ya ——.

406. I want to reserve a room.

Θέλω νὰ κρατήσω ἕνα δωμάτιο.

THEH-lo na-kra-TEE-so EH-nah tho-MA-tee-o.

407. I want a room with (without) meals.

Θέλω ἕνα δωμάτιο μετὰ (ἄνευ) φαγητοῦ.

THEH-lo EH-na tho-MA-tee-o meh-TA (AH-nef) fa-yee-TOO.

408. I want a (single, double) room.

Θέλω ἕνα δωμάτιο (μὲ ἕνα κρεβάτι, μὲ δύο κρεβάτια).

THEH-lo EH-na tho-MA-tee-o (meh EH-na kreh-VA-tee, meh THEE-o kreh-VA-tya).

409. A room with a double bed.

Ἕνα δωμάτιο μὲ διπλὸ κρεβάτι.

EH-na tho-MA-tee-o meh thee-PLO kreh-VA-tee.

410. Single bed.   Twin beds.

Μονὸ κρεβάτι.   Διπλᾶ κρεβάτια.

mo-NO kreh-VA-tee.   thee-PLA kreh-VA-tya.

411. A suite.   With (bath, shower).

Διαμέρισμα.   Μὲ (μπάνιο, ντούζ).

thee-ah-MER-eez-ma.   meh (BAH-nyo, DOOZ).

412. With a window (a balcony).

Μέ παράθυρο (μπαλκόνι).

meh pa-RA-thee-ro (bal-KO-nee).

413. For —— days.   For tonight.

Γιὰ —— μέρες.   Γι' ἀπόψε.

ya —— MEH-ress.   ya-PO-pseh.

414. For —— persons.
Γιά —— ἄτομα.
ya —— AH-to-ma.

415. What is the rate per day?
Πόσο εἶναι τὸ ἐνοίκιο τὴν ἡμέρα;
PO-so EE-neh toh eh-NEE-kee-o teen ee-MER-ah?

416. Are tax and room service included?
Συμπεριλαμβάνονται ὁ φόρος καὶ ἡ ὑπηρεσία;
seem-beh-ree-lahm-VA-nohn-deh o FO-rohss keh ee ee-pee-reh-SEE-ah?

417. A week. A month.
Ἑβδομάδα. Μήνας.
ev-tho-MA-thah. MEE-nass.

418. On what floor. Stairs.
Σὲ ποιὸ πάτωμα. Σκάλες.
se-PYO PA-to-ma. SKA-less.

419. Upstairs. Downstairs.
Ἐπάνω. Κάτω.
eh-PA-no. KA-toh.

420. Is there an elevator?
Ἔχει ἀσανσέρ;
EH-khee ah-sahn-SER?

421. Running water. Hot water.
Τρεχούμενο νερό. Ζεστὸ νερό.
treh-KHOO-meh-no neh-RO. zest-O neh-RO.

422. I want a front (back) room.

Θέλω ἕνα δωμάτιο μπροστινὸ (πίσω μέρος).

THEH-lo EH-nah tho-MA-tee-o bro-stee-NO (PEE-so MEH-rohss).

423. On a lower floor.   Higher up.

Στὸ κάτω πάτωμα.   Πιὸ ἐπάνω.

sto KA-toh PA-toh-ma.   PYO eh-PA-no.

424. I should like to see the room.

Θὰ ἤθελα νὰ δῶ τὸ δωμάτιο.

thah EE-theh-la na-THO toh tho-MA-tee-o.

425. I (do not) like this one.

(Δὲν) μοῦ ἀρέσει αὐτό.

(then) moo ah-RESS-ee ahf-TOH.

426. Have you something better?

Ἔχετε κανένα καλύτερο;

EH-khe-te ka-NEH-na ka-LEE-teh-ro?

427. Cheaper.

Φθηνότερο.

fthee-NO-teh-ro.

428. With more light (air).

Μὲ περισσότερο φῶς (ἀέρα).

meh peh-ree-SO-teh-ro FOHSS (ah-ER-ah).

429. Larger.   Smaller.

Μεγαλύτερο.   Μικρότερο.

meh-gha-LEE-teh-ro.   mee-KRO-teh-ro.

430. Please sign the hotel register.

Παρακαλῶ ὑπογράψτε τὸ βιβλίο ἀπο-
γραφῆς.

*pah-ra-ka-LO ee-po-GHRAP-steh toh vee-
VLEE-o ah-po-ghra-FEESS.*

431. I have baggage at the station.

Ἔχω πράγματα στὸ σταθμό.

EH-kho PRAGH-ma-ta sto sta-THMO.

432. Will you send for my bags?

Παρακαλῶ στεῖλτε γιὰ τὶς βαλίτσες μου.

*pah-ra-ka-LO STEE-lteh ya teess va-LEE-
tsez-moo.*

433. Here is the check for my trunk.

Ὁρίστε ἡ ἀπόδειξη γιὰ τὸ μπαοῦλό μου.

*or-EE-steh ee ah-PO-thee-ksee ya toh bah-OO-
lo-moo.*

434. Please send bath towels to my room.

Παρακαλῶ στεῖλτέ μου πετσέτες τοῦ
προσώπου στὸ δωμάτιό μου.

*pa-ra-ka-LO STEEL-teh-moo peh-TSEH-
tess too pro-SO-poo sto tho-MA-tee-O-moo.*

435. Washcloths.

Μικρὲς πετσέτες γιὰ σαπούνισμα.

*mee-KRESS peh-TSEH-tess ya sa-POO-neez-
ma.*

436. Face towels.

Πετσέτες τοῦ προσώπου.

peh-TSEH-tess too pro-SO-poo.

437. Ice. Ice water.

Πάγος. Νερὸ τοῦ πάγου.

PA-ghohss. neh-RO too PA-ghoo.

438. Boy (Messenger). Room service.

Παιδί. Ὑπηρεσία δωματίων.

peh-THEE. ee-pee-ress-EE-a tho-ma-TEE-ohn.

439. How much should I tip the maid?

Πόσο νὰ τῆς δώσω τῆς ὑπηρέτριας;

PO-so na tees THO-so teess ee-pee-RET-ree-ass?

440. Please call me at —— o'clock.

Παρακαλῶ φωνάξτε με στὶς ——.

pa-ra-ka-LO fo-NAK-stem-eh steess ——.

441. I want breakfast in my room.

Θέλω πρόγευμα στὸ δωμάτιό μου.

THEH-lo PRO-yev-ma sto tho-MA-tee-o-moo.

442. Could I have some laundry done?

Θὰ μποροῦσα νὰ δώσω κάμποσα ροῦχα
νὰ πλυθοῦν;

*tha bo-ROO-sa na-THO-so KAM-bo-sa
ROO-kha na-plee-THOON?*

443. I want these things pressed.

Θέλω νὰ τὰ δώσω αὐτὰ νὰ σιδηρωθοῦν.

THEH-lo na ta THO-so af-TA na-see-thee-ro-THOON.

444. I should like to speak to the manager.

Θὰ ἤθελα νὰ μιλήσω στὸ διευθυντή.

theh EE-theh-la na-mee-LEE-so sto thee-ef-theen-DEE.

445. My room key, please.

Τὸ κλειδὶ τοῦ δωματίου μου, παρακαλῶ.

toh klee-THEE too tho-ma-TEE-oo-moo, pa-ra-ka-LO.

446. Have I any letters or messages?

Ἔχω γράμματα ἤ σημειώσεις;

EH-kho GHRA-ma-ta ee see-mee-O-seess?

447. Is the linen furnished?

Θὰ μοῦ δώσετε σεντόνια;

thah moo THO-seh-teh send-O-nya?

448. How much is it a month?

Πόσο ἔχει τὸ μῆνα;

PO-so EH-khee toh MEE-nah?

449. Blankets.   The silver.   Dishes.

Κουβέρτες.   Μαχαιροπήρουνα.   Πιάτα.

*koo-VER-tess.   ma-kher-o-PEE-roo-na.
PYA-tah.*

450. Do you know a good cook (a good maid)?

Ξέρετε κανέναν καλὸ μάγειρα (καμιὰ καλὴ ὑπηρέτρια);

KSEH-reh-teh kahn-EH-nan-ga-LO MA-yee-ra (ka-mya-ka-LEE ee-pee-RET-ree-ah)?

451. Where can I rent a garage?

Ποὺ μπορῶ νὰ ἐνοικιάσω γκαράζ;

POO bo-RO na-eh-nee-kee-AH-so ga-RAHZ?

RESTAURANT

454. Where is there a good restaurant?
Ποῦ ἔχει καλὸ ἐστιατόριο;
POO EH-khee ka-LO ess-tee-ah-TOR-ee-o?

455. Breakfast.   Lunch or Dinner.
Πρόγευμα. Γεῦμα.
PRO-yev-ma.   YEV-ma.

456. Supper.   A sandwich.   A snack.
Δεῖπνο. Σάντουιτς. Κολατσιό.
T̄HEE-pnoh. SAND-oo-eets. ko-la-TSYO.

457. At what time is dinner served?
Τὶ ὥρα σερβίρεται τὸ γεῦμα;
TEE OR-ah ser-VEE-ret-eh toh YEV-ma?

458. Can we lunch (or dine) now?
Μποροῦμε νὰ φᾶμε τώρα;
bo-ROO-meh na-FA-meh TOR-ah?

459. The waitress.   The waiter.
Ἡ σερβιτόρα. Ὁ σερβιτόρος.
ee ser-vee-TOR-ah.   o ser-vee-TOR-ohss.

460. Waiter!   The headwaiter.
Γκαρσόν! Ὁ ἀρχισερβιτόρος.
gar-SOHN!   o ar-khee-ser-vee-TOR-ohss.

461. There are two (five) of us.
Εἴμαστε δύο (πέντε).
EE-mass-teh T̄HEE-o (PEN-deh).

462. Give me a table inside (outside, near the window).

Δῶστέ μου ἕνα τραπέζι μέσα (ἔξω, σιμὰ στὸ παράθυρο).

THO-steh-moo EH-na tra-PEH-zee MEH-sa (EK-so, see-MA sto pa-RA-thee-ro).

463. At the side.   In the corner.

Στὸ πλάϊ. Στὴ γωνία.

sto PLAH-ee.   stee gho-NEE-ah.

464. Is this table reserved?

Εἶναι αὐτὸ τὸ τραπέζι κρατημένο;

EE-neh ahf-TOH toh tra-PEH-zee kra-tee-MEH-no?

465. That one will be free soon.

Αὐτὸ θὰ εἶναι ἐλεύθερο σύντομα.

ahf-TOH tha EE-neh eh-LEF-theh-ro SEEN-do-ma.

466. Where can I wash up?

Ποῦ μπορῶ νὰ πλυθῶ;

POO bo-RO na-plee-THO?

467. Please serve us quickly.

Παρακαλῶ σερβίρατέ μας γρήγορα.

pa-ra-ka-LO ser-VEE-ra-TEH-mass GHREE-gho-ra.

468. We want to dine à la carte.

Θέλομε νὰ φᾶμε ἀλὰ κάρτ.

THEH-lo-meh na-FA-meh a-la-KART.

469. What do you recommend?

Τὶ μοῦ συνιστᾶτε νὰ φάω;

TEE moo seen-ee-STA-teh na FA-o?

470. Bring me the menu (wine list).

Φέρτε μου τὸν κατάλογο τῶν φαγητῶν (τὸν κατάλογο τῶν κρασιῶν).

FER-teh-moo tohn-ga-TA-lo-gho tohn fa-yee-TOHN (tohn-ga-TA-lo-gho tohn kra-SYOHN).

471. A plate. Πιάτο. *PYA-toh.*

472. A knife. Μαχαίρι. *ma-KHER-ee.*

473. A fork. Πιρούνι. *pee-ROO-nee.*

474. A large spoon. Κουτάλι. *koo-TA-lee.*

475. A teaspoon. Κουταλάκι. *koo-ta-LA-kee.*

476. The bread. Τὸ ψωμί. *toh pso-MEE.*

477. The butter. Τὸ βούτυρο. *toh VOO-tee-ro.*

478. The cream. Ἡ ἀφρόκρεμα. *ee ahf-RO-kreh-mah.*

479. The sugar. Ἡ ζάχαρη. *ee ZA-kha-ree.*

480. The salt. Τὸ ἁλάτι. *toh ah-LA-tee.*

481. The pepper. Τὸ πιπέρι. *toh pee-PER-ee.*

482. The sauce. Ἡ σάλτσα. *ee SAHL-tsa.*

483. The oil. Τὸ λάδι. *toh LA-thee.*

484. The vinegar. Τὸ ξίδι. *toh KSEE-thee.*

485. This is not clean.

Αὐτὸ δὲν εἶναι καθαρό.

ahf-TOH then EE-neh ka-tha-RO.

486. A (little) more of this.

(Λίγο) ἀκόμη ἀπὸ αὐτό.

(LEE-gho) ah-KO-mee ah-po ahf-TOH.

487. I have had enough, thanks.

Εἶχα ἀρκετό, εὐχαριστῶ.

EE-kha ahr-keh-TOH, ef-kha-reess-TOH.

488. I want something simple.

Θέλω κάτι ἁπλό.

THEH-lo KA-tee ah-PLO.

489. Not too spicy.

Ὄχι πολύ καρυκευμένο.

O-khee po-LEE kar-ee-kev-MEH-no.

490. I like the meat cooked rare (well done, broiled, baked, fried).

Τὸ κρέας μοῦ ἀρέσει ὄχι πολύ βρασμένο (καλὰ ψημένο, τῆς σκάρας, ψητό, τηγανιτό).

toh KREH-ass moo-ah-RESS-ee O-khee po-LEE vraz-MEH-no (ka-LA psee-MEH-no, teess SKAR-ass, psee-TOH, tee-gha-nee-TOH).

491. This is overcooked.

Αὐτὸ εἶναι πολύ βρασμένο.

ahf-TOH EE-neh po-LEE vraz-MEH-no.

492. This is undercooked.

Αὐτὸ δὲν εἶναι καλὰ βρασμένο.

ahf-TOH then EE-neh ka-LA vrahz-MEH-no.

493. This is too tough (sweet, sour).

Αὐτὸ εἶναι πολύ σκληρό (γλυκό, ξυνό).

ahf-TOH EE-neh po-LEE sklee-RO (ghlee-KO, ksee-NO).·

494. This is cold.
　Αὐτὸ εἶναι κρύο.
　ahf-TOH EE-neh KREE-o.

495. Take it away, please.
　Πάρτε το ἀπὸ δῶ, παρακαλῶ.
　PART-et-o ah-po-THO, pah-ra-ka-LO.

496. I did not order this.
　Δὲν τὸ παρήγγειλα αὐτό.
　then toh par-EEN-gee-la ahf-TOH.

497. May I change this for ——?
　Μπορῶ νὰ τὸ ἀλλάξω αὐτὸ γιὰ ——;
　bo-RO na toh ah-LA-kso ahf-TOH ya ——?

498. May I see your pastries?
　Μπορῶ νὰ δῶ τὰ γλυκά σας;
　bo-RO na THO ta-ghlee-KA-sass?

499. Ask the headwaiter to come here.
　Πέστε τὸν ἀρχισερβιτόρο νὰ ἔλθη ἐδῶ.
　*PESS-te tohn ar-khee-ser-vee-TOR-o nah-EL-
　thee eh-THO.*

500. The check please.
　Τὸ λογαριασμὸ παρακαλῶ.
　toh lo-gha-ryaz-MO pa-ra-ka-LO.

501. Is the tip included?
　Συμπεριλαμβάνεται τὸ μπουρμπουάρ;
　seem-per-eel-ahm-VA-neh-teh toh-boor-boo-AR?

502. Is the service charge included?
　Συμπεριλαμβάνεται ἡ ὑπηρεσία;
　*seem-per-eel-ahm-VA-neh-teh ee ee-pee-ress-EE-
　ah?*

503. What are these charges for?

Γιὰ τὸ τί μοῦ τὰ χρειώνετε αὐτά;

ya toh TEE moo-ta-khree-OH-neh-teh ahf-TAH?

504. There is a mistake in the bill.

Εἶναι ἕνα λάθος στὸ λογαριασμό.

EE-neh EH-na LA-thohss sto lo-gha-ryahz-MO.

505. Keep the change.

Κρατῆστε τὰ ρέστα.

krah-TEE-steh ta-RESS-ta.

506. Kindly pay at the cashier's.

Σᾶς παρακαλῶ πληρῶστε στὸ ταμεῖο.

sass pa-ra-ka-LO plee-RO-steh sto tah-MEE-o.

CAFÉ

510. Bartender.   A glass of ——.

Μπάρμαν. Ἕνα ποτήρι ——.

BAR-mahn.   EH-na po-TEE-ree ——.

511. A drink.   A liqueur.   A carbonated

Πιοτό.   Λικέρ.   Γκαζόζα.   **[soda.**

pyo-TOH.   lee-KER.   ga-ZO-za.

512. Liquor store.   Coffee shop.   Tavern.

Ποτοπωλεῖο.   Καφενεῖο.   Ταβέρνα.

po-to-po-LEE-o. ka-feh-NEE-o. ta-VER-nah.

513. A small (large) bottle of ——.

Ἕνα μικρὸ (μεγάλο) μπουκάλι ——.

EH-na meek-RO (meh-GHA-lo) boo-KA-lee

514. Beer.   Wine (red, white).

Μπύρα.   Κρασὶ (κόκκινο, ἄσπρο).

BEE-ra.   krah-SEE (KO-kee-no, ASS-pro).

515. Retsina

[a popular Greek light wine containing some resin as a preservative].

Ρετσίνα.

reh-TSEE-nah.

516. Ouzo

[an anise-flavoured hard liquor which is the favorite apéritif in Greece].

Οὖζο.

OO-zo.

517. Whiskey (and soda).

Οὐΐσκυ (καὶ σόδα).

oo-EE-skee (keh SO-da).

518. Cognac.   Champagne.

Κονιάκ.   Σαμπάνια.

ko-NYAK.   sahm-BAH-nyah.

519. To your health.

Στὴν ὑγειά σας.

steen-ee-YA-sass.

520. Let's have another.

(Ἄς πιοῦμε) ἀκόμη ἕνα.

(ass-PYOO-meh) ah-KO-mee EH-nah.

CHURCH

523. Where is there a service in English?

Ποῦ ἔχει ἐκκλησία ἀγγλική;

POO EH-khee eh-klee-SEE-ah ahn-glee-KEE?

524. A Catholic church.

Καθολικὴ ἐκκλησία.

ka-tho-lee-KEE eh-klee-SEE-ah.

525. A Protestant church.

Διαμαρτυρομένη ἐκκλησία.

thee-a-mar-tee-ro-MEH-nee eh-klee-SEE-a.

526. A synagogue.

Συναγωγή.

see-na-gho-YEE.

527. When is the service (mass)?

Πότε ἔχει ἐκκλησία (λειτουργία);

PO-teh EH-khee eh-klee-SEE-ah (lee-toor-YEE-ah)?

528. Is there an English-speaking priest (rabbi)?

Εἶναι κανένας παπὰς (ραβίνος) ποὺ νὰ μιλᾶ ἀγγλικά;

EE-neh ka-NEH-nass pah-PAHSS (ra-VEE-nohss) poo na-mee-LA ahn-glee-KA?

SIGHTSEEING

530. I want to hire a car.

Θέλω νὰ ἐνοικιάσω ἕνα αὐτοκίνητο.

THEH-lo na-eh-nee-kee-AH-so EH-na ahf-toh-KEE-nee-toh.

531. I want a guide who speaks English.

Θέλω ἕναν ὁδηγὸ ποὺ νὰ μιλᾶ ἀγγλικά.

THEH-lo EH-nahn oh-thee-GHO poo na-mee-LA ahn-glee-KA.

532. Call for me tomorrow at my hotel at 9 o'clock.

Φωνάξτε με αὔριο στὶς ἐννέα στὸ ξενοδοχεῖο.

fo-NAK-stem-eh AHV-ree-o steess eh-NEH-a sto ksen-o-tho-KHEE-o.

533. What is the charge per hour (day)?

Πόσο χρειώνετε τὴν ὥρα (ἡμέρα);

PO-so khree-OH-neh-teh teen OR-ah (ee-MER-ah)?

534. How much do you want for the whole trip?

Πόσο θέλετε γιὰ ὅλο τὸ ταξίδι;

PO-so THEH-leh-teh ya O-lo toh ta-KSEE-thee?

535. Please show me all the sights of interest.

Παρακαλῶ δεῖξτέ μου ὅλα τὰ ἀξιοθέατα.

pa-ra-ka-LO THEEK-stem-oo O-la ta ah-ksee-oh-THEH-ah-ta.

536. I am interested in archeology.

'Ενδιαφέρομαι γιὰ τὴν ἀρχαιολογία.

ehn-thee-ah-FER-o-meh ya teen ahr-kheh-o-lo-YEE-ah.

537. Native arts and crafts.

'Ελληνικὴ λαϊκὴ τέχνη.

eh-lee-nee-KEE lah-ee-KEE TEKH-nee.

538. Architecture. Ruins.

'Αρχιτεκτονικὴ. Τὰ ἀρχαῖα.

ahr-khee-tek-toh-nee-KEE. ta ahr-KHEH-ah.

539. Painting. Sculpture.
Ζωγραφική. Γλυπτική.
zo-ghra-fee-KEE. ghlee-ptee-KEE.

540. Shall I have time to visit the museums?
Θὰ ἔχω καιρὸ νὰ ἐπισκεφθῶ τὰ μουσεῖα;
thah EH-kho keh-RO na eh-pee-skef-THO tah moo-SEE-ah?

541. How long does it take to walk?
Πόσο θὰ μᾶς πάρη νὰ βαδίσωμε;
PO-so thah mass PAR-ee na-va-$\overline{THEE}$-so-meh?

542. The cathedral. The monastery.
'Η μητρόπολις. Τὸ μοναστήρι.
ee mee-TRO-po-leess. toh mo-na-STEE-ree.

543. The temple. The castle. The island.
'Ο ναός. Τὸ κάστρο. Τὸ νησί.
o nah-OHSS. toh KA-stro. toh nee-SEE.

544. Is it (still) open?
Εἶναι (ἀκόμη) ἀνοικτό;
EE-neh (ah-KO-mee) ah-neek-TOH?

545. We want to stop for refreshments.
Θέλομε νὰ σταματήσωμε γιὰ ἀναψυκτικά.
THEH-lo-meh na-sta-ma-TEE-so-meh ya ah-na-psee-ktee-KA.

546. How long must I wait?
Πόσο πρέπει νὰ περιμένω;
PO-so PREH-pee na-per-ee-MEH-no?

547. Where is the entrance (exit)?

Ποῦ εἶναι ἡ εἴσοδος (ἔξοδος);

POO EE-neh ee EE-so-thohss (EK-so-thohss)?

548. What is the price of admission?

Ποία εἶναι ἡ τιμὴ τοῦ εἰσιτηρίου;

PEE-ah EE-neh ee tee-MEE too ee-see-tee-REE-oo?

549. Do we need an interpreter?

Χρειαζόμαστε διερμηνέα;

khree-ah-ZO-ma-steh thee-er-mee-NEH-ah?

550. How much is the guide book?

Πόσο ἔχει ὁ ὁδηγός;

PO-so EH-khee o oh-thee-GHOHSS?

551. May I take photographs?

Μπορῶ νὰ πάρω φωτογραφίες;

bo-RO na-PA-ro fo-to-ghra-FEE-ess?

552. We want to stop for postcards (souvenirs).

Θέλομε νὰ σταματήσωμε γιὰ κάρτες (ἐνθύμια).

THEH-lo-meh nah-sta-ma-TEE-so-meh ya KAR-tess (en-THEE-mee-ah).

553. Do you have a book in English about ——?

Ἔχετε κανένα βιβλίο στὰ ἀγγλικὰ γιὰ ——;

EH-kheh-teh ka-NEH-na vee-VLEE-o sta ahn-glee-KA ya——?

554. Take me back to the hotel.
Ὁδηγῆστέ με πίσω στὸ ξενοδοχεῖο.
oh-thee-YEE-stem-eh PEE-so sto ksen-o-tho-KHEE-o.

555. Let's go back by way of the market place.
Πᾶμε ἀπὸ τὴν ἀγορά.
PA-meh ah-po teen ah-gho-RA.

AMUSEMENTS

558. Balcony. Ὑπερῷον. *ee-per-OH-ohn.*

559. Ballet. Μπαλέτο. *ba-LET-o.*

560. Beach. Ἀκτὴ or πλάζ.
ahk-TEE or PLAHZ.

561. Box. Θεωρεῖο. *theh-or-EE-o.*

562. Box office. Ταμεῖο. *ta-MEE-o.*

563. Café. Καφέ. *ka-FEH.*

564. Concert. Συναυλία. *see-nahv-LEE-ah.*

565. Cover charge. Κουβέρ. *koo-VER.*

566. Fishing. Ψάρεμα. *PSA-reh-ma.*

567. Folk dances. Ἑλληνικοὶ χοροί.
eh-lee-nee-KEE kho-REE.

568. Gambling casino. Καζίνο. *ka-ZEE-no.*

569. Golf. Γκόλφ. *GOLF.*

570. Horseracing. Ἱπποδρόμιο.
ee-po-THRO-mee-o.

571. Movies. Κινηματογράφος.
kee-nee-ma-toh-GHRA-fohss.

572. Night club. Καμπαρέ. *ka-ba-REH.*

573. Opera. Μελόδραμα. *meh-LO-dra-ma.*

574. Opera glasses. Κυάλια. *KYA-lyah.*

575. Orchestra seat. Θέση πλατείας.
THEH-see pla-TEE-ass.

576. Program. Πρόγραμμα.
PRO-ghra-mah.

577. Reserved seat. Κρατημένη θέση.
krah-tee-MEH-nee THEH-see.

588. Skating. Παγοδρομία or πατινάζ.
pa-gho-thro-MEE-ah or pa-tee-NAHZ.

589. Skiing. Σκί. *SKEE.*

590. Soccer. Φουτμπόλ. *foot-BOHL.*

591. Swimming. Κολύμπι. *ko-LEEM-bee.*

592. Tennis. Τένις. *TEN-eess.*

593. Theatre. Θέατρο. *THEH-ah-tro.*

594. Where can we go to dance?
Ποῦ μπορούμε νὰ πᾶμε νὰ χορέψωμε;
POO bo-ROO-meh nah-PA-meh nah-kho-REP-so-meh?

595. May I have this dance?
Μπορῶ νὰ ἔχω αὐτὸ τὸ χορό;
bo-RO na-EH-kho ahf-TOH toh-kho-RO?

596. Is there a matinee today?
Ἔχει ἀπογευματινὴ σήμερα;
EH-khee ah-po-yev-ma-tee-NEE SEE-mer-ah?

597. When does the (evening) performance start?

Πότε ἀρχίζει ἡ (βραδυνὴ) παράσταση;

PO-teh ahr-KHEE-zee ee (vra-$\overline{thee}$-NEE) pa-RA-sta-see?

598. Can you please play a foxtrot (rumba, tango, waltz)?

Μπορεῖτε νὰ παίξετε σᾶς παρακαλῶ ἕνα φοξτρότ (μία ρούμπα, ἕνα ταγκό, ἕνα βάλς).

bo-REE-teh na-PEK-seh-teh sass-pa-ra-ka-LO EH-na-fohks-TROT (MEE-ah ROO-ba, EH-nah tahn-GO, EH-nah VAHLS)?

599. Have you any seats for tonight?

Ἔχετε θέσεις γι' ἀπόψε;

EH-kheh-teh THEH-seess ya-PO-pseh?

600. Can I see (hear) well from there?

Μπορῶ νὰ ἰδῶ (ἀκούσω) καλὰ ἀπὸ ἐδῶ;

bo-RO nah-ee-$\overline{THO}$ (ah-KOO-so) ka-LA ah-po eh-$\overline{THO}$?

601. Not too near (far).

Ὄχι πολὺ κοντὰ (μακρυά).

O-khee po-LEE ko(hn)-DA (ma-kree-AH).

602. The music is excellent.

Ἡ μουσικὴ εἶναι ὑπέροχη.

ee moo-see-KEE EE-neh ee-PER-o-khee.

603. This is very interesting (funny).

Αὐτὸ εἶναι πολὺ ἐνδιαφέρον (ἀστεῖο).

ahf-TOH EE-neh po-LEE ehn-thee-ah-FER-ohn (ass-TEE-o).

604. Is this the intermission?

Εἶναι (τὸ) διάλειμα;

EE-neh(toh) thee-AH-lee-ma?

SHOPPING

(Becáuse of the difference between Puristic (the official language) and Demotic (the standard spoken and literary language), we consider it useful to give in parentheses the name of the stores in Puristic, written in CAPITAL letters exactly as they appear on signs, whenever they differ from those used in the spoken language.)

607. I want to go shopping.

Θέλω νὰ πάω νὰ ψωνίσω.

THEH-lo na-PA-o na-pso-NEE-so.

608. Please drive me around the shopping center.

Παρακαλῶ, μὲ πηγαίνετε στὰ κεντρικὰ καταστήματα;

pa-ra-ka-LO, meh-pee-YEN-eh-teh sta kehn-dree-KA ka-ta-STEE-ma-tah?

609. I am just looking around.

Ἁπλῶς κοιτάζω.

ahp-LOSS kee-TAH-zo.

610. May I speak to a male (female) sales clerk?

Μπορῶ νὰ ὁμιλήσω σ' ἕναν (σὲ μία) ὑπάλληλο;

bo-RO na - o - mee - LEE - so SEH - nahn (se-MEE-ah) ee-PAH-lee-lo?

611. Is there an English-speaking person here?

Εἶναι κανεὶς ἐδῶ ποὺ νὰ μιλᾶ ἀγγλικά;

EE-neh kah-NEESS eh-THO poo nah-mee-LA ahn-glee-KA?

612. Where is the bakery (pastry shop)?

Ποῦ εἶναι ὁ φοῦρνος (τὸ ζαχαροπλαστεῖο);

POO EE-neh o FOOR-nohss (toh za-kha-ro-plass-TEE-o)?

613. Antique shop. Ἀντίκες.   *ahn-DEE-kess.*

614. Bookshop. Βιβλιοπωλεῖο.

vee-vlee-o-po-LEE-o.

615. Candy store. Ζαχαροπλαστεῖο.

za-kha-ro-plass-TEE-o.

616. Cigar store. Καπνοπωλεῖο.

ka-pno-po-LEE-o.

617. Clothing store. Ἐμπορικό.

ehm-bo-ree-KO.

618. Department store.

Κατάστημα νεωτερισμῶν.

ka-TA-stee-ma neh-o-ter-eez-MOHN.

619. Dressmaker. Μοδίστρα.

mo-THEESS-tra.

620. Drug store. Φαρμακεῖο.   *far-ma-KEE-o.*

621. Grocery.

Μπακάλικο (ΠΑΝΤΟΠΩΛΕΙΟΝ).

ba-KA-lee-ko (pahn-doh-po-LEE-ohn).

622. Hardware store.

Κατάστημα σιδηρικῶν.

ka-TA-stee-ma see-thee-ree-KOHN.

623. Hat shop. Καπελάδικο (ΠΙΛΟΠΟΙΕΙΟΝ).

ka-peh-LA-thee-ko (pee-lo-pee-EE-ohn).

624. Jewelry store. Χρυσοχοεῖο.

khree-so-kho-EE-o.

625. Meat market.

Χασάπικο (ΚΡΕΟΠΩΛΕΙΟΝ).

kha-SA-pee-ko (kreh-o-po-LEE-ohn).

626. Shoe store.

Τσαγγάρικο (ΥΠΟΔΗΜΑΤΟΠΟΙΕΙΟΝ).

tsa-GAR-ee-ko (ee-po-thee-ma-to-pee-EE-ohn).

627. Shoemaker. Τσαγγάρης or παπουτσής.

tsahn-GAR-eess or pa-poo-TSEESS.

628. Tailorshop. Ραφεῖο. *ra-FEE-o.*

629. Toy shop. Ψιλικά. *psee-lee-KA.*

630. Watchmaker. Ὡρολογοποιός.

or-o-lo-gho-pee-OHSS.

631. Please regulate my watch for me.

Παρακαλῶ κανονίστε τὸ ρολόϊ μου.

pa-ra-ka-LO ka-no-NEE-steh toh-ro-LO-ee-moo.

632. How much will it cost to have it repaired?

Πόσο θὰ μοῦ κοστίση νὰ τὸ ἐπιδιορθώσω;

PO-so thah moo ko-STEE-see na toh eh-pee-thee-or-THO-so?

633. Sale. Bargain sale.
Πώλησις. Ξεπούλημα.
PO-lee-seess. kseh-POO-lee-ma.

634. I (do not) like that.
(Δὲν) μοῦ ἀρέσει αὐτό.
(then) moo-ah-RESS-ee ahf-TOH.

635. I want to buy.
Θέλω νὰ ψωνίσω.
THEH-lo na-pso-NEE-so.

636. How much is it all together?
Πόσα ἔχουν ὅλα μαζί;
PO-sa EH-khoon O-la ma-ZEE?

637. How much is it for each piece?
Πόσο ἔχει τὸ ἕνα;
PO-so EH-khee toh EH-na?

638. It is very expensive.
Εἶναι πολὺ ἀκριβό.
EE-neh po-LEE ah-kree-VO.

639. You said it would cost ——.
Εἴπατε ὅτι θὰ κοστίση ——.
EE-pa-teh O-tee tha ko-STEE-see ——.

640. I prefer something better (cheaper).
Προτιμῶ κάτι καλύτερο (φθηνότερο).
pro-tee-MO KA-tee ka-LEE-teh-ro (fthee-NO-teh-ro).

641. Finer. Καλύτερο. *ka-LEE-teh-ro.*

642. Stronger. Γερώτερο. *yeh-RO-teh-ro.*

643. Larger. Μεγαλύτερο.
meh-gha-LEE-teh-ro.

644. Smaller.   Μικρότερο.   *mee-KRO-teh-ro.*

645. Longer.   Μακρύτερο.   *ma-KREE-teh-ro.*

646. Shorter.   Κοντότερο.
kohn-DOH-teh-ro.

647. Wider or **Looser.**   Φαρδύτερο.
far-$\overline{THEE}$-teh-ro.

648 Narrower or **Tighter.**   Στενώτερο.
steh-NO-teh-ro.

649. Heavier.   Βαρύτερο.   *va-REE-teh-ro.*

650. Thinner.   Ψιλότερο.   *psee-LO-teh-ro.*

651. Thicker.   Χονδρότερο.
khon-DRO-teh-ro.

652. Lighter.   Ἐλαφρότερο.
eh-laff-RO-teh-ro.

653. Show me some others.
Δεῖξτέ μου μερικὰ ἄλλα.
$\overline{THEEK}$-st͙e-oo meh-ree-KA AH-la.

654. May I try this one?
Μπορῶ νὰ τὸ δοκιμάσω;
bo-RO na toh $\overline{tho}$-kee-MAH-so?

655. Can I order one?
Μπορῶ νὰ παραγγείλω ἕνα;
bo-RO na pa-rann-GEE-lo EH-na?

656. When shall I call for it?
Πότε νὰ ἔλθω νὰ τὸ πάρω;
PO-teh na EL-tho na toh PA-ro?

657. How long will it take?
Πότε θὰ τὸ ἔχετε ἕτοιμο;
PO-teh tha toh EH-kheh-teh EH-tee-mo?

658. Can you have it ready for this evening?

Μπορεῖτε νὰ τὸ ἑτοιμάσετε γι' ἀπόψε;

bo-REE-teh na toh eh-tee-MA-seh-teh ya-PO-pseh?

659. Please take my measurements.

Παρακαλῶ πάρτε τὰ μέτρα μου.

pa-ra-ka-LO PAR-teh ta MET-ra-moo.

660. It does not fit me.

Δὲν μοῦ γίνεται.

then moo YEE-neh-teh.

661. It is (not) becoming to me.

(Δὲν) μοῦ πηγαίνει.

(then) moo pee-YEN-ee.

662. Will this fade (shrink)?

Θὰ ξεβάψη (μαζεύση);

tha kseh-VA-psee (ma-ZEF-see)?

663. Will you wrap this please?

Μοῦ τὸ τυλίγετε παρακαλῶ;

moo toh tee-LEE-yeh-teh pa-ra-ka-LO?

664. I will take it with me.

Θὰ τὸ πάρω μαζί μου.

tha toh PA-ro ma-ZEE-moo.

665. Can you ship it to me by freight?

Μπορεῖτε νὰ μοῦ τὸ στείλετε;

bo-REE-teh na moo toh STEE-leh-teh?

666. Where do I pay?

Ποῦ θὰ πληρώσω;

POO tha plee-RO-so?

667. Please bill me.

Παρακαλῶ χρεῶστέ με.

pa-ra-ka-LO khreh-O-stem-eh.

668. Are there any other charges (delivery charges)?

Εἶναι τίποτε ἄλλα ἔξοδα (ἔξοδα διανομῆς);

EE-neh TEE-po-teh AH-la EK-so-t͞ha (EK-so-t͞ha t͞hee-ah-no-MEESS)?

669. Let me have a sales slip.

Μοῦ δίδετε ἀπόδειξη πωλήσεως.

moo-T͞HEE-t͞heh-teh ah-PO-t͞heek-see po-LEE-seh-ohss.

670. You will be paid on delivery.

Θά πληρωθῆτε ὅταν μοῦ τό στείλετε.

tha-plee-ro-T͞HEE-teh O-tahn moo toh STEE-leh-teh.

671. This parcel is fragile (perishable), please be careful.

Αὐτό τό δέμα εἶναι εὔθραυστο (εὐκολό-φθαρτο), παρακαλῶ προσέξτε.

ahf-TOH toh T͞HEH-ma EE-neh EF-thraf-sto (ef-ko-LOHF-thar-toh), pa-ra-ka-LO pro-SEK-steh.

672. Pack this carefully for export.

Πακετάρητέ το προσεκτικά γιά ἐξαγωγή.

pa-ket-AR-ee-TEH-toh pro-sek-tee-KA ya ek-sa-gho-YEE.

POST OFFICE

673. Where is the post office?
Πού είναι τὸ ταχυδρομεῖο;
POO EE-neh toh ta-khee-thro-MEE-o?

674. To which window do I go?
Σὲ ποιά θυρίδα νὰ πάω;
se-PYA thee-REE-tha na-PA-o?

675. Postcard. Κάρτα. *KAR-ta.*

676. Letter. Γράμμα. *GHRA-ma.*

677. By airmail. ᾽Αεροπορικῶς.
ah-eh-ro-po-ree-KOHSS.

678. Parcel post. Ταχυδρομικὸ δέμα.
ta-khee-thro-mee-KO THEH-mah.

679. General delivery. Πὸστ ρεστάντ.
post-rest-AHNT.

680. Registered. Συστημένο.
see-stee-MEH-no.

681. Special delivery. ᾽Επεῖγον.
eh-PEE-ghohn.

682. Insured. ᾽Ασφαλισμένο.
ass-fa-leez-MEH-no.

683. Three stamps of —— drachmas.
Τρία γραμματόσημα —— δραχμῶν.
TREE-ah ghra-ma-TOH-see-ma —— thrakh-MOHN.

684. I want to send a money order.

Θέλω νὰ στείλω μία ἐπιταγή.

THEH-lo na-STEE-lo MEE-ah eh-pee-ta-YEE.

685. There is nothing dutiable on this.

Δὲν ἔχει τίποτε φορολογήσιμο.

then EH-khee TEE-po-teh fo-ro-lo-YEE-see-mo.

686. Will this go out today?

Θὰ σταλῆ σήμερα;

tha-sta-LEE SEE-meh-rah?

687. Give me a receipt, please.

Δῶστε μου μία ἀπόδειξη, παρακαλῶ.

THO-steh-moo MEE-ah ah-PO-theek-see, pa-ra-ka-LO.

688. "To await arrival."

Νὰ κρατηθῆ μέχρι ἀφίξεως.

na-kra-tee-THEE MEH-khree ah-FEEK-seh-ohss.

BANK

694. Where is the nearest bank?

Ποῦ εἶναι ἡ πλησιέστερη τράπεζα;

POO EE-neh ee plee-see-ESS-teh-ree TRA-peh-za?

695. I want to send fifty dollars to the U.S.

Θέλω νὰ στείλω πενήντα δολλάρια στὰς
'Ηνωμένας Πολιτείας.

*THEH-lo na-STEE-lo peh-NEEN-da t͞ho-
LA-ree-ah stass ee-no-MEH-nass po-lee-
TEE-ass.*

696. At which window can I cash this?

Σὲ ποιὰ θυρίδα μπορῶ νὰ τὸ ἐξαργυρώσω
αὐτό;

*se-PYA thee-REE-t͞ha bo-RO na toh ek-sar-
yee-RO-so ahf-TOH?*

697. Can you change this for me?

Μπορεῖτε νὰ μοῦ τὸ ἀνταλλάξετε αὐτό;

*bo-REE-teh na moo toh ahn-da-LA-kseh-teh
ahf-TOH?*

698. Will you cash a check?

Θὰ μοῦ ἐξαργυρώσετε μία ἐπιταγή;

*tha moo ek-sar-yee-RO-seh-teh MEE-ah eh-
pee-ta-YEE?*

699. Do not give me large bills.

Μὴ μοῦ δίνετε μεγάλα χαρτονομίσματα.

*mee moo T͞HEE-neh-teh meh-GHA-la khar-
toh-no-MEEZ-ma-ta.*

700. May I have some change?

Μπορῶ νὰ ἔχω λίγα ψιλά;

bo-RO nah-EH-kho LEE-gha psee-LA?

701. I have traveller's checks.

῍Εχω ἐπιταγὲς ταξιδιωτῶν.

EH-kho eh-pee-ta-YES ta-ksee-t͞hee-oh-TOHN.

702. Letter of credit.

Πιστωτικὴ ἐπιστολή.

pee-stoh-tee-KEE eh-pee-stoh-LEE.

703. Bank draft.

Τραπεζιτικὴ ἐντολή.

tra-peh-zee-tee-KEE ehn-do-LEE.

704. What is the exchange rate on the dollar?

Ποιὰ εἶναι ἡ τιμὴ ἀνταλλαγῆς τοῦ δολλαρίου;

PYA EE-neh ee tee-MEE ahn-da-la-YEESS too tho-la-REE-oo?

BOOKSTORE AND STATIONER'S

705. Where is there a bookshop?

Ποῦ ἔχει βιβλιοπωλεῖο;

POO EH-khee vee-vlee-o-po-LEE-o?

706. Can you recommend a book about ——?

Μπορεῖτε νὰ μοῦ συστήσετε ἕνα βιβλίο γιὰ ——;

bo-REE-teh na moo see-STEE-seh-teh EH-na vee-VLEE-o ya——?

707. I want a map of Greece.

Θέλω ἕνα χάρτη τῆς Ἑλλάδος.

THE-lo EH-na KHAR-tee teess eh-LA-thohss.

708. A stationer's.   Χαρτοπωλεῖο.

khar-toh-po-LEE-o.

709. A newsdealer. Ἐφημεριδοπώλης.

eh-fee-meh-ree-tho-PO-leess.

710. Artist's materials.
Ὑλικὰ καλλιτέχνου.
ee-lee-KAH ka-lee-TEKH-noo.

711. Book. Βιβλίο.   vee-VLEE-o.

712. Blotter. Στυπόχαρτο.
stee-PO-khar-toh.

713. Carbon paper. Χημικό.
khee-mee-KO.

714. Dictionary. Λεξικό.   leh-ksee-KO.

715. Envelopes (airmail).
Φάκελα (ἀεροπορικά).
FA-kel-ah (a-e-ro-po-ree-KA).

716. Eraser. Κομπολάστιχα.
kohm-bo-LA-stee-kha.

717. Fountain pen. Στυλό (γράφος).
stee-LO(GHRA-fohss).

718. Greeting cards. Κάρτες.   KAR-tess.

719. Guide book. Ὁδηγός.   oh-thee-GHOHSS.

720. Ink. Μελάνη.   meh-LA-nee.

721. Magazines. Περιοδικά.   per-ee-o-thee-KA.

722. Newspapers. Ἐφημερίδες.
eh-fee-meh-REE-thess.

723. Pencil. Μολύβι.   mo-LEE-vee.

724. Playing cards. Χαρτιά.   khar-TYA.

725. Postcards. Κάρτες.   KAR-tess.

726. Scotch tape. Κορδέλα κολλήματος.
kor-THEH-la ko-LEE-ma-tohss.

727. String. Σχοινί. *skhee-NEE.*

728. Tissue paper. Χαρτί γιὰ τὸ μέρος.
khar-TEE ya toh MEH-rohss.

729. Typewriter ribbon.
Κορδέλα (γραφομηχανῆς).
kor-THEH-la (ghra-fo-mee-kha-NEESS).

730. Wrapping paper.
Χαρτί (περὶ) τυλίγματος.
khar-TEE (per-ee) tee-LEEGH-ma-tohss.

731. Writing paper. Χαρτί γραψίματος.
khar-TEE ghrap-SEE-ma-tohss.

CIGAR STORE

732. Where is the nearest cigar store?
Ποῦ εἶναι τὸ πλησιέστερο καπνοπωλεῖο;
POO EE-neh toh plee-see-ESS-teh-ro ka-pno-po-LEE-o?

733. I want some cigars.
Θέλω λίγα ποῦρα.
THEH-lo LEE-gha POO-ra.

734. A pack of American cigarettes, please.
Ἕνα πακέτο ἀμερικανικὰ σιγαρέττα, παρακαλῶ.
EH-na pa-KET-o ah-mer-ee-ka-nee-KA see-gha-REH-ta, pah-ra-ka-LO.

735. Please show me some cigarette cases.

Παρακαλῶ δεῖξτέ μου μερικὲς ταμπακέρες.

*pa-ra-ka-LO THEEK-stem-oo meh-ree-KESS
ta(hm)-ba-KER-ess.*

736. I need a lighter.

Θέλω ἕναν ἀναπτῆρα.

THEH-lo EH-nahn ah-na-PTEE-ra.

737. May I have a match (light), please?

Μπορῶ νὰ ἔχω ἕνα σπίρτο (φωτιά),
παρακαλῶ;

*bo-RO na-EH-kho EH-na SPEER-toh (fo-
TYA), pa-ra-ka-LO?*

738. Flint. Τσακμακόπετρα.

tsak-ma-KO-pet-ra.

739. Fluid. Βενζίνη. *ven-ZEE-nee.*

740. Matches. Σπίρτα. *SPEER-ta.*

741. Pipe. Πίπα. *PEE-pa.*

742. Pipe tobacco. Καπνὸ τῆς πίπας.

kahp-NO teess PEE-pahs.

743. Pouch. Σακούλα γιὰ καπνό.

sa-KOO-la ya kap-NO.

BARBER SHOP AND BEAUTY PARLOR

744. Where is there a good barber?

Ποῦ ἔχει καλὸ κουρεῖο;

POO EH-khee ka-LO koo-REE-o?

745. I want a (haircut, shave).

Θέλω (νὰ κόψω τὰ μαλλιά, νὰ ξυρισθῶ).

THEH-lo (na-KO-pso ta ma-LYA, na-ksee-reess-THO).

746. Not too short.

Ὄχι πολὺ κοντά.

OH-khee po-LEE kohn-DA.

747. Do not cut any off the top.

Μὴν τὰ κόβετε μπροστά.

meen ta KO-veh-teh bro-STA.

748. Do not put on oil.

Μὴ βάζετε λάδι.

mee VA-zeh-teh LA-thee.

749. I part my hair on the other side.

Κάνω τὴ χωρίστρα ἀπὸ τὸ ἄλλο μέρος.

KA-no tee kho-REESS-tra ah-po toh AH-lo MEH-rohss.

750. In the middle.

Στὴ μέση.

stee-MEH-see.

751. The water is too hot (cold).

Τὸ νερὸ εἶναι πολὺ ζεστὸ (κρύο).

toh neh-RO EE-neh po-LEE zest-O (KREE-o).

752. I want my shoes shined.

Θέλω νὰ γυαλίσω τὰ παπούτσια μου.

THEH-lo na-ya-LEE-so ta pa-POO-tsya-moo.

753. May I make an appointment with you for tomorrow?

Μπορῶ νὰ σᾶς συναντήσω αὔριο;
bo-RO na sahss seen-ahn-DEE-so AV-ree-o?

754. I should like a new hair style.

Θὰ ἤθελα νὰ μοῦ κάνετε τὰ μαλλιά μου διαφορετικά.
tha EE-theh-la na moo KA-neh-teh ta ma-LYA-moo thee-ah-fo-reh-tee-KA.

755. I want to have my hair tinted.

Θέλω νὰ βάψω τὰ μαλλιά μου.
THEH-lo na-VA-pso ta ma-LYA-moo.

756. May I see the color samples?

Μπορῶ νὰ δῶ τὰ δείγματα τῶν χρωμάτων;
bo-RO na-THO ta THEEGH-ma-ta tohn khro-MA-tohn?

757. A finger wave.

᾽Οντολασιὸν or μιζανπλί.
ohn-do-la-SYOHN or meez-ahn-PLEE.

758. A permanent.

Περμανάντ.
per-mahn-AHNT.

759. A manicure.

Μανικιούρ.
ma-nee-KEWR.

760. A facial.

Μασάζ τοῦ προσώπου.
ma-SAHZ too pro-SO-poo.

761. Where can I see a chiropodist?

Ποῦ μπορῶ νὰ δῶ ἕναν εἰδικὸ γιὰ τοὺς κάλους;

POO bo-RO na-THO EH-nahn ee-thee-KO ya tooss KA-looss?

PHOTOGRAPHY

762. I want a roll of (color) film.

Θέλω ἕνα (χρωματιστὸ) φίλμ.

THEH-lo   EH-nah   (khro-ma-teess-TOH) FEELM.

763. The size is ——.

Τὸ μέγεθος εἶναι ——.

toh MEH-ye-thohss EE-neh ——.

764. For this camera.

Γι' αὐτὴ τὴ φωτογραφικὴ μηχανή.

yaf-TEE tee fo-to-ghra-fee-KEE mee-kha-NEE.

765. Movie film.

Κινηματογραφικὴ ταινία.

kee-nee-ma-toh-ghra-fee-KEE teh-NEE-ah.

766. Flashbulb.

Φλάς.

FLAHS.

767. What is the charge for developing a roll?

Πόσο θὰ κοστίση νὰ μοῦ ἐμφανίσ ετε τὸ φίλμ;

PO-so tha-ko-STEE-see na moo ehm-fa-NEE-seh-teh toh FEELM?

768. For one print of each.

Γιὰ κάθε ἐκτύπωση.

ya KA-theh ek-TEE-po-see.

769. For an enlargement.

Γιὰ μεγέθυνση.

ya meh-YEH-theen-see.

770. When will they be ready?

Πότε θὰ εἶναι ἔτοιμα;

PO-teh tha-EE-neh EH-tee-ma?

771. The camera is out of order.

'Η φωτογραφικὴ μηχανὴ δὲν ἐργάζεται.

ee fo-to-ghraf-ee-KEE mee-kha-NEE then er-GHA-zet-eh.

772. Do you rent cameras?

'Ενοικιάζετε φωτογραφικὲς μηχανές;

eh-nee-kee-AH-zet-eh fo-to-ghraf-ee-KESS mee-kha-NESS?

773. I should like one for today.

Θὰ ἤθελα μία γιὰ σήμερα.

tha EE-theh-la MEE-ah ya SEE-meh-ra.

774. Would you mind letting me take your picture?

Μοῦ ἐπιτρέπετε νὰ σᾶς πάρω φωτογραφία;

moo eh-pee-TREH-peh-teh na sass PA-ro fo-to-ghraf-EE-ah?

LAUNDRY AND DRY CLEANING

775. Where is the nearest laundry (dry cleaner)?

Ποῦ εἶναι τὸ πλησιέστερο πλυντήριο (καθαριστήριο);

POO EE-neh toh plee-see-ESS-teh-ro pleen-DEE-ree-o (ka-tha-reess-TEE-ree-o)?

776. I want this shirt to be washed (mended).

Θέλω νὰ δώσω αὐτὸ τὸ πουκάμισο νὰ πλυθῆ (νὰ μανταρισθῆ).

THEH-lo na-THO-so ahf-TOH toh-poo-KA-mee-so na-plee-THEE (na-mahn-da-reess-THEE).

777. Can you have this suit cleaned (pressed)?

Μπορεῖτε νὰ δώσετε αὐτὸ τὸ κοστούμι νὰ καθαρισθῆ (σιδερωθῆ);

bo-REE-teh na-THO-seh-teh ahf-toh toh ko-STOO-mee na-ka-thar-eess-THEE (see-ther-o-THEE)?

778. Do not wash this in hot water.

Μὴ τὸ πλένετε αὐτὸ σὲ ζεστὸ νερό.

mee toh PLEN-et-eh ahf-toh seh zest-O neh-RO.

779. Use lukewarm water.

Χρησιμοποιεῖστε χλιαρὸ νερό.

khree-see-mo-pee-EESS-teh khlee-ar-O neh-RO.

780. Be careful about this (these).

Προσέξτε αὐτὸ (αὐτά).

pro-SEK-steh ahf-TOH (ahf-TA).

781. Remove this stain.

Βγάλτε αὐτὸ τὸ λεκέ.

VGHAL-teh ahf-TOH toh-leh-KEH.

782. Do not dry this in the sun.

Μὴ τὸ στεγνώνετε στὸν ἥλιο.

mee toh stegh-NO-neh-teh stohn EE-lee-o.

783. Do not starch the collars.

Μὴ τοὺς βάλετε στὴν κόλλα τοὺς γιακάδες.

*mee tooss VA-leh-teh steen-GO-la tooss ya-KA-
  $\overline{th}$ess.*

784. Starch the collars.

Κολλαρίστε τοὺς γιακάδες.

ko-lar-EESS-teh tooss ya-KA-$\overline{th}$ess.

785. When can I have this?

Πότε μπορῶ νὰ τὸ ἔχω;

PO-teh bo-RO na toh EH-kho?

786. The belt is missing.

῾Η ζώνη λείπει.

ee ZO-nee LEE-pee.

CLOTHING

787. Apron.   Ποδιά.   *po-$\overline{TH}YA$.*

788. Bathing cap.   Σκούφια γιὰ τὸ μπάνιο.

SKOO-fya ya toh BA-nyo.

789. Bathing suit. Μπανιερό. *ba-nyer-O.*

790. Blouse. Μπλούζα. *BLOO-za.*

791. Brassière. Σοτιέν. *So-TYEN.*

792. Coat. Σακάκι. *sa-KA-kee.*

793. Collar. Γιακάς. *ya-KASS.*

794. Collar pin. Παραμάνα τοῦ γιακᾶ.
pa-ra-MA-na too ya-KA.

795. Cuff links. Κουμπιά γιὰ τὰ μανικέτια.
koom-BYA ya ta ma-nee-KET-ya.

796. Diapers. Πάνες γιὰ μωρά.
PA-ness ya mor-AH.

797. Dress. Φόρεμα. *FOR-eh-ma.*

798. Garters. Καλτσοδέτες.
kahl-tso-THEH-tess.

799. Girdle. Κορσές. *kor-SESS.*

800. Gloves. Γάντια. *GHAHN-dya.*

801. Handkerchief. Μαντήλι.
mahn-DEE-lee.

802. Hat. Καπέλο. *ka-PEH-lo.*

803. Jacket. Ζακέτα. *za-KET-ah.*

804. Necktie. Γραβάτα. *ghra-VA-ta.*

805. Nightgown. Νυκτικό. *neek-tee-KO.*

806. Overcoat. Παλτό. *pahl-TOH.*

807. Pajamas. Πιτζάμα. *pee-DZA-ma.*

808. Panties. Κυλότα. *kee-LO-ta.*

809. Petticoat. Μεσοφόρι. *meh-so-FO-ree.*

810. Raincoat. 'Αδιάβροχο.
ah-thee-AHV-ro-kho.

811. Robe. Ρόμπα. *ROHM-ba.*

812. Sandals (beach). Πέδιλα (σάνδαλα).
PEH-thee-la (SAHN-da-la).

813. Scarf. Κασκόλ. *kass-KOL.*

814. Shirt. Πουκάμισο. *poo-KA-mee-so.*

815. Shoes. Παπούτσια. *pa-POO-tsya.*

816. Shorts. Κοντά παντελόνια.
kohn-DA pahn-deh-LO-nya.

817. Skirt. Φούστα. *FOO-sta.*

818. Slacks. Παντελόνια. *pahn-deh-LO-nya.*

819. Slip. Κομπιναιζόν. *kohm-bee-neh-ZON.*

820. Slippers. Παντόφλες. *pahn-DOH-fless.*

821. Socks. Κάλτσες (ἀνδρικές).
KAL-tsess (ahn-dree-KESS).

822. Sport shirt. Φανέλα. *fah-NEH-la.*

823. Stockings (nylon). Κάλτσες (νάϊλον).
KAL-tsess (NA-ee-lohn).

824. Suit (man's). Κοστούμι. *ko-STOO-mee.*

825. Suit (woman's). Ταγιέρ. *ta-YER.*

826. Suspenders. Τιράντες. *tee-RAHN-dess.*

827. Sweater. Ζελέ. *zeh-LEH.*

828. Trousers. Παντελόνια.
pahn-deh-LO-nya.

829. Undershirt. Φανέλα (ἐσωτερική).
fa-NEH-la (eh-so-ter-ee-KEE).

830. Underwear.   Ἐσώρρουχα.
eh-SO-roo-kha.

831. Vest.   Γελέκο.   *ye-LEH-ko.*

HEALTH AND ACCIDENTS

832. There has been an accident.
Ἔγινε δυστύχημα.
EH-yee-neh t̄heess-TEE-khee-ma.

833. Get a doctor (nurse).
Φέρτε ἕνα γιατρὸ (μία νοσοκόμο).
FER-teh EH-na ya-TRO (MEE-ah no-so-KO-mo).

834. Send for an ambulance.
Στεῖλτε γιὰ νοσοκομειακὸ αὐτοκίνητο.
STEEL-teh ya no-so-ko-mee-ah-KO ahf-toh-KEE-nee-toh.

835. Please bring blankets.
Παρακαλῶ φέρτε κουβέρτες.
pa-ra-ka-LO FER-te koo-VER-tess.

836. A stretcher.   Water.
Φορεῖο.   Νερό.
fo-REE-o.   neh-RO.

837. He is (seriously) injured.
Εἶναι (σοβαρὰ) τραυματισμένος.
EE-neh (so-va-RA) trav-ma-teez-MEH-nohss.

838. Help me lift him.
Βοηθῆστέ με νὰ τὸν σηκώσω.
vo-ee-THEE-stem-eh na tohn see-KO-so.

839. He was hit.

Χτυπήθηκε.

khtee-PEE-thee-ke.

840. She has fallen (has fainted).

Αὐτὴ ἔπεσε (λυποθύμησε).

ahf-TEE EH-peh-seh (lee-po-THEE-mee-seh).

841. I feel weak.

Αἰσθάνομαι ἀδυναμία.

ess-THA-no-meh ah-thee-na-MEE-ah.

842. He has a fracture.

Ἔχει κάταγμα.

EH-khee KA-tagh-ma.

843. He has a bruise (cut).

Μωλωπίστηκε (κόπηκε).

mo-lo-PEE-stee-keh (KO-pee-keh).

844. He has burned (cut) his hand.

Ἔκαψε (ἔκοψε) τὸ χέρι του.

EH-ka-pseh (EH-ko-pseh) toh-KHER-ee-too.

845. It is bleeding.

Τρέχει αἷμα.

TREH-khee EH-ma.

846. It is swollen.

Εἶναι πρησμένο.

EE-neh preez-MEH-no.

847. Can you dress this?

Μπορεῖτε νὰ τὸ δέσετε αὐτό;

bo-REE-teh na toh THEH-seh-teh ahf-TOH?

848. Have you any bandages (or splints)?

Ἔχετε ἐπιδέσμους;

EH-kheh-teh eh-pee-$\overline{THEZ}$-mooss?

849. I need something for a tourniquet.

Θέλω κάτι γιὰ αἱμοστατικὸ ἐπίδεσμο.

THEH-lo KA-tee ya eh-mo-sta-tee-KO eh-PEE-$\overline{th}$ez-mo.

850. Are you all right?

Εἴσθε ἐν τάξει;

EESS-theh ehn-DA-ksee?

851. It hurts here.

Μοῦ πονεῖ ἐδῶ.

meh po-NEE eh-$\overline{THO}$.

852. I want to sit down a moment.

Θέλω νὰ καθίσω μιὰ στιγμή.

THEH-lo na-ka-THEE-so mya steegh-MEE.

853. I cannot move my ——.

Δὲν μπορῶ νὰ κινήσω τὸ ——.

$\overline{th}$en bo-RO na-kee-NEE-so toh ——.

854. I have hurt my ——.

Χτύπησα τὸ ——.

KHTEE-pee-sa toh ——.

See PARTS OF THE BODY, page 98.

855. Please notify my husband (wife, friend).

Παρακαλῶ εἰδοποιεῖστε τὸν ἄντρα μου (τὴ γυναίκα μου, τὸ φίλο μου).

pa-ra-ka-LO ee-$\overline{th}$o-pee-EESS-teh tohn AHN-dra-moo (tee yee-NEH-ka-moo, toh-FEE-lo-mo).

856. Here is my identification (my card).

Ὁρίστε ἡ ταυτότητά μου (ἡ κάρτα μου).

or-EESS-teh ee taf-TOH-tee-ta-moo (ee KAR-ta-moo).

857. I have broken (lost) my glasses.

Ἔσπασα (ἔχασα) τὰ γυαλιά μου.

ESS-pa-sa (EH-kha-sa) ta-ya-LYA-moo.

858. Where can I find an optometrist (or optician)?

Ποῦ μπορῶ νὰ βρῶ ἕναν ὀφθαλμολόγο;

POO   bo-RO na-VRO   EH-nahn off-thal-mo-LO-gho?

859. Who can fix this hearing aid?

Ποιὸς μπορεῖ νὰ μοῦ διορθώση τὸ ἀκουστικό;

PYOHSS bo-REE na moo t̄hee-or-THO-see toh ah-koo-stee-KO?

ILLNESS

860. I wish to see a doctor (specialist).

Θέλω νὰ δῶ ἕνα γιατρὸ (εἰδικό).

THEH-lo na-T̄HO EH-na ya-TRO (ee-t̄hee-KO).

861. An American doctor.

Ἕναν ἀμερικανὸ γιατρό.

EH-nahn ah-meh-ree-ka-NO ya-TRO.

862. I do not sleep well.

Δὲν κοιμοῦμαι καλά.

t̄hen kee-MOO-meh ka-LA.

863. My foot hurts.

Τὸ πόδι μου πονεῖ.

toh-PO-thee-moo po-NEE.

864. My head aches.

Ἔχω πονοκέφαλο.

EH-kho po-no-KEH-fa-lo.

865. I have a virus.

Μολύνθηκα.

mo-LEEN-thee-ka.

866. Can you give me something to relieve my allergy?

Μπορεῖτε νὰ μοῦ δώσετε κάτι νὰ ἀνακου-φίσω τὴν ἀλλεργία μου;

bo-REE-teh na moo THO-seh-teh KA-tee na ah-na-koo-FEE-so teen ah-ler-YEE-ah-moo?

867. Appendicitis. Σκωληκοειδῖτις.
sko-lee-ko-ee-THEE-teess.

868. A bite. Δάγκωμα.   *THAHN-go-ma.*

869. An insect bite. Τσίμπημα ἐντόμου.
TSEEM-bee-ma ehn-DOH-moo.

870. A blister. Φουσκάλα.   *foo-SKA-la.*

871. A boil. Ζεμάτισμα.   *zeh-MA-teez-ma.*

872. A burn. Κάψιμο.   *KAH-psee-mo.*

873. Chills. Ρίγη.   *REE-ghee.*

874. A cold. Κρύο.   *KREE-o.*

875. Chafed. Ἐρεθισμένο.   *eh-reh-theez-MEH-no.*

876. Constipation. Δυσκοιλιότης.   *theess-kee-lee-O-teess.*

877. A cough. Βήχας.   *VEE-khass.*

878. A cramp. Σπασμός.   *spaz-MOHSS.*

879. Diarrhoea. Διάρροια.   *thee-AR-ee-ah.*

880. Dysentery. Δυσεντερία.   *thee-sen-der-EE-ah.*

881. An earache. Πόνος στὸ αὐτί.   *PO-nohss sto ahf-TEE.*

882. **A fever.** Πυρετός. *pee-reh-TOHSS.*

883. **Food poisoning.** Δηλητηρίασις ἀπὸ τρόφιμα. *thee-lee-tee-REE-ah-seess ah-po TRO-fee-ma.*

884. **Hoarseness.** Βράχνας. *VRAKH-nass.*

885. **Indigestion.** Δυσπεψία. *theess-pep-SEE-ah.*

886. **Nausea.** Ναυτία. *nahf-TEE-ah.*

887. **Pneumonia.** Πνευμονία. *pnev-mo-NEE-ah.*

888. **Sore throat.** Πονόλαιμος. *po-NO-leh-mohss.*

889. **Sprain.** Ἐξάρθρωσις. *ek-SAR-thro-seess.*

890. **Sunburn.** Ἡλιοκαύματα. *ee-lee-o-KAV-ma-ta.*

891. **Sunstroke.** Ἡλίασις. *ee-LEE-ass-eess.*

892. **Typhoid fever.** Τυφοειδὴς πυρετός. *tee-fo-ee-THEESS pee-reh-TOHSS.*

893. **To vomit.** Νὰ κάνω μετό. *na-KA-no met-O.*

894. What am I to do?

Τὶ πρέπει νὰ κάνω;
TEE PREH-pee na-KA-no?

895. Must I stay in bed?

Πρέπει νὰ μείνω στὸ κρεβάτι;
PREH-pee na-MEE-no sto kreh-VA-tee?

896. Do I have to go to a hospital?

Πρέπει νὰ πάω στὸ νοσοκομεῖο;
PREH-pee na-PA-o sto no-so-ko-MEE-o?

897. May I get up?

Μπορῶ νὰ σηκωθῶ;
bo-RO na-see-ko-THO?

898. I feel better.

Αἰσθάνομαι καλύτερα.
ess-THA-no-meh ka-LEE-teh-ra.

899. When do you think I'll be better?

Πότε νομίζετε θὰ εἶμαι καλύτερα;

PO-teh no-MEE-zeh-te tha EE-meh ka-LEE-teh-ra?

900. Can I travel on Monday?

Μπορῶ νὰ ταξιδεύσω τὴ Δευτέρα;

bo-RO na-ta-ksee-$\overline{THEV}$-so tee $\overline{thef}$-TEH-ra?

901. When will you come again?

Πότε θὰ ξαναέλθετε;

PO-teh thah ksa-na-EL-theh·teh?

902. Please write out a medical bill.

Παρακαλῶ γράψτε τὸ λογαριασμό.

pa-ra-ka-LO　GHRAP-steh　toh-lo-ghar-yahz-MO.

903. A drop. Στάλα. *STAH-la.*

904. A teaspoonful.

Κουταλάκι (τοῦ τσαγιοῦ).

koo-ta-LA-kee (too tsa-YOO).

905. Medicine. Φάρμακο. *FAR-ma-ko.*

906. Twice a day. Δύο φορὲς τὴν ἡμέρα.

$\overline{THEE}$-o for-ESS teen ee-MEH-ra.

907. Hot water. Ζεστὸ νερό. *zest-O neh-RO.*

908. Ice. Πάγος. *PA-ghohss.*

909. A pill. Χάπι. *KHA-pee.*

910. A prescription. Συνταγή. *seen-da-YEE.*

911. Every hour. Κάθε ὥρα. *KA-theh OR-ah.*

912. Before meals. Πρὸ τοῦ φαγητοῦ.

pro too fa-yee-TOO.

913. After meals.   Μετὰ τὸ φαγητό.
meh-ta toh fa-yee-TOH.

914. On going to bed.
῞Οταν πηγαίνετε νὰ κοιμηθῆτε.
O-tahn   pee-YEN-eh-teh   na-kee-mee-THEE-teh.

915. On getting up.   ῞Οταν σηκώνεσθε.
O-tahn see-KO-ness-theh.

916. X-rays.   ᾿Ακτῖνες.   *ah-KTEE-ness.*

See also DRUG STORE, page 95.

DENTIST

917. Do you know a good dentist?
Ξέρετε κανέναν καλὸν ὀδοντογιατρό;
KSEH-reh-teh   ka-NEH-nahn-ga-LOHN   o-thohn-doh-ya-TRO?

918. This tooth hurts.
Αὐτὸ τὸ δόντι πονεῖ.
ahf-TOH toh THOHN-dee po-NEE.

919. Can you fix it temporarily.
Μπορεῖτε νὰ τὸ διορθώσετε προσωρινά;
bo-REE-teh na toh thee-or-THO-seh-teh pro-so-ree-NA?

920. I have lost a filling.
Μοῦ ἔπεσε ἕνα σφράγισμα.
moo EH-peh-seh EH-na SFRA-yeez-ma.

921. I have an abscess.
Ἔχω ἀπόστημα.
EH-kho ah-PO-stee-ma.

922. I have broken a tooth.
Μοῦ ἔσπασε ἕνα δόντι.
moo ESS-pa-seh EH-na $\overline{THOHN}$-dee.

923. I (do not) want it extracted.
(Δὲν) θέλω νὰ τὸ βγάλω.
($\overline{then}$) THEH-lo na toh VGHA-lo.

924. Can you save it?
Μπορεῖτε νὰ τὸ σώσετε;
bo-REE-teh no toh SO-seh-teh?

925. You are hurting me.
Μὲ πονεῖτε.
meh po-NEE-teh.

926. Can you repair this denture?
Μπορεῖτε νὰ ἐπισκευάσετε αὐτὴ τὴν μασέλα;
bo-REE-teh na eh-pee-skev-AH-seh-teh ahf-TEE teen ma-SEH-la?

927. Local anesthesia.
Τοπικὴ ἀναισθητικὴ ἔνεση.
toh-pee-KEE ah-ness-thee-tee-KEE EH-ness-ee.

928. The gums.   The nerve.
Τὰ οὖλα.   Τὸ νεῦρο.
ta OO-la.   toh NEV-ro.

DRUG STORE

929. Where is there a drug store where they understand English?

Ποῦ ἔχει φαρμακεῖο ποὺ καταλαβαίνουν ἀγγλικά;

POO EH-khee far-ma-KEE-o poo ka-ta-la-VEN-oon ahn-glee-KA?

930. Can you fill this prescription?

Μπορεῖτε νὰ ἐκτελέσετε αὐτὴ τὴ συνταγή;

bo-REE-teh na ek-te-LESS-eh-teh ahf-TEE tee seen-da-YEE?

931. How long will it take?

Σὲ πόση ὥρα θὰ εἶναι ἔτοιμο;

seh PO-see OR-ah tha EE-neh EH-tee-mo?

932. Can you deliver it to this address?

Μπορεῖτε νὰ τὸ στείλετε σ' αὐτὴν τὴ διεύθυνση;

bo-REE-teh na toh STEE-leh-teh sahf-TEEN tee thee-EF-theen-see?

933. I want adhesive tape.

Θέλω τσιρότο.

THEH-lo tsee-RO-toh.

934. Alcohol. Οἰνόπνευμα. *ee-NO-pnev-ma.*

935. Antiseptic. Ἀντισηπτικό. *ahn-dee-see-ptee-KO.*

936. Aspirin. Ἀσπιρίνη. *ah-spee-REE-nee.*

937. Analgesic. Ἀναλγητικό. *ah-nal-yee-tee-KO.*

938. Bandages. Ἐπίδεσμοι. *eh-PEE-thez-mee.*

939. Bicarbonate of soda. Σόδα. *SO-tha.*

940. Boric acid. Βορικὸ ὀξύ. *vo-ree-KO o-KSEE.*

941. **A hair brush.** Βούρτσα γιὰ τὰ μαλλιά.
VOOR-tsa ya ta ma-LYA.

942. **A tooth brush.** 'Οδοντόβουρτσα. *o-thohn-DO-voor-tsa.*

943. **Carbolic acid.** Φανικὸ ὀξύ. *fah-nee-KO o-KSEE.*

944. **Castor oil.** Ρετσινόλαδο. *ret-seen-O-la-tho.*

945. **A comb.** Τσατσάρα. *tsa-TSA-ra.*

946. **Corn pads.** Τσιρότα γιὰ τοὺς κάλους.
tsee-RO-ta ya tooss KA-looss.

947. **Cotton.** Βαμβάκι. *vahm-BA-kee.*

948. **A depilatory.** Ντεπιλατουάρ.
deh-pee-la-too-AR.

949. **A deodorant.** 'Απολυμαντικό. *ah-po-lee-mahn-dee-KO.*

950. **Ear stoppers.** Προφυλακτῆρες τῶν αὐτιῶν.
pro-fee-lak-TEE-ress tohn ahf-TYOHN.

951. **Epsom salts.** 'Αλάτι τῆς 'Ιγγλατέρας.
ah-LA-tee teess een-gla-TER-ass.

952. **An eyecup.** Κουπάκι γιὰ τὸ μάτι.
koo-PA-kee ya toh MA-tee.

953. **Face cream** or **Cold cream.** Κρέμα προσώπου.
KREH-ma pro-SO-poo.

954. **Face tissues.** Τουαλέτας χαρτί.
too-a-LET-ass khar-TEE.

955. **A gargle.** Γαργάρα. *ghar-GHA-ra.*

956. **Gauze.** Γάζα. *GHA-zah.*

957. **Hot water bottle.** Θερμοστάτης. *ther-mo-STA-teess.*

958. **Ice bag.** Σακούλα γιὰ τὸν πάγο.
sa-KOO-la ya tohn PA-gho.

959. **Insecticide.** 'Εντομοκτόνο. *en-doh-mo-KTO-no.*

960. **Iodine.** 'Ιώδιο. *ee-O-thee-o.*

961. **A laxative (mild).** Καθαρτικὸ (ἐλαφρό).
ka-thar-tee-KO (eh-laff-RO).

962. **Lipstick.** Κραγιόν. *kra-YON.*

963. **Medicine dropper.** Σταγονόμετρο.
sta-gho-NO-met-ro.

964. **Mouthwash.** 'Αντισηπτικὸ γιὰ τὸ στόμα.
ahn-dee-see-ptee-KO ya toh STO-mα.

965. **Nail file.** Λίμα γιὰ τὰ νύχια.
LEE-ma ya ta NEE-khya.

966. Nail polish (remover). Βαφή γιὰ τὰ νύχια.
va-FEE ya ta NEE-khya.

967. Peroxide. 'Οξυζενέ. *o-ksee-zeh-NEH.*

968. Powder. Πούδρα. *POO-thra.*

969. Poison. Δηλητήριο. *thee-lee-TEE-ree-o.*

970. Quinine. Κινίνο. *kee-NEE-no.*

971. Razor. Ξυράφι. *ksee-RA-fee.*

972. Razor blades. Ξυραφάκια or λάμες.
ksee-ra-FA-kya or *LA-mess.*

973. Rouge. Ρούζ. *rooz.*

974. Sanitary napkins. Απολυμασμένες πετσέτες.
ah-po-lee-maz-MEH-ness peh-TSEH-tess.

975. Sedative. χαταπραϋντικό. *ka-ta-prah-een-dee-KO.*

976. Shampoo (liquid, cream).
Σαμπουάν (ὑγρό, κρέμα).
sahm-boo-AHN (ee-GHRO, KREH-ma).

977. Shaving lotion.
Κολόνια ξυρίσματος.
ko-LO-nya ksee-REEZ-ma-tohss.

978. Shaving cream (brushless).
Κρέμα ξυρίσματος (χωρὶς πινέλο).
KREH-ma ksee-REEZ-ma-tohss (kho-REESS pee-NEH-lo).

979. Soap. Σαπούνι. *sa-POO-nee.*

980. Sunburn ointment. Κρέμα γιὰ τὰ ἡλιοκαύματα.
KREH-ma ya ta ee-lee-o-KAV-ma-ta.

981. Smelling salts. 'Αμμωνιακὰ ἅλατα.
ah-mo-nee-ah-KA AH-la-ta.

982. Suntan oil. Λάδι γιὰ τὰ ἡλιοκαύματα.
LA-thee ya ta ee-lee-o-KAV-ma-ta.

983. Thermometer. Θερμόμετρο. *ther-MO-met-ro.*

984. Toilet tissue. Τουαλέτας χαρτί.
too-ah-LET-ass khar-TEE.

985. Toothpaste. 'Οδοντόκρεμα. *o-thohn-DO-kreh-ma.*

986. Toothpowder. Σκόνη γιὰ τὰ δόντια.
SKO-nee ya ta THOHN-dya.

PARTS OF THE BODY

987 Appendix.   Ἀπόφυσις.   *ah-PO-fee-seess.*

988 Arm.   Μπράτσο.   *BRA-tso.*

989. Back.   Πλάτη.   *PLA-tee.*

990. Blood.   Αἷμα.   *EH-ma.*

991. Bone.   Κόκαλο.   *KO-ka-lo.*

992. Breast.   Στήθη.   *STEE-thee.*

993. Cheek.   Μάγουλο.   *MA-ghoo-lo.*

994. Chest.   Στῆθος.   *STEE-thohss.*

995. Chin.   Σαγόνι.   *sa-GHO-nee.*

996. Collar bone.   Κλειδοκόκαλο.   *klee-tho-KO-ka-lo.*

997. Ear.   Αὐτί.   *af-TEE.*

998. Elbow.   Ἀγκώνας.   *an-GO-nahs.*

999. Eye.   Μάτι.   *MA-tee.*

1000. Eyebrows.   Φρύδια.   *FREE-thya.*

1001. Eyelashes.   Ματοτσύνουρα.   *ma-toh-TSEE-noo-ra.*

1002. Eyelid.   Βλέφαρο.   *VLE-fa-ro.*

1003. Face.   Πρόσωπο.   *PRO-so-po.*

1004. Finger.   Δάκτυλο.   *THA-ktee-lo.*

1005. Foot.   Πόδι.   *PO-thee.*

1006. Forehead.   Μέτωπο.   *MEH-to-po.*

1007. Hair.   Μαλλιά.   *ma-LYA.*

1008. Hand.   Χέρι.   *KHEH-ree.*

1009. Head.   Κεφάλι.   *keh-FA-lee.*

1010. Heart.   Καρδιά.   *kar-THYA.*

1011. Heel.   Πτέρνα.   *PTER-na.*

1012. Hip.   Γοφός.   *gho-FOHSS.*

1013. Intestines.   Ἐντόσθια.   *ehn-DO-sthee-ah.*

1014. Jaw.   Σιαγόνα.   *see-a-GHO-na.*

1015. Joint.   Κλείδωση.   *KLEE-tho-see.*

1016. Kidney.   Νεφρό.   *neh-FRO.*

1017. Knee.   Γόνατο.   *GHO-na-toh.*

1018. **Leg.** Γάμπα and μπούτι. *GHAHM-ba* and *BOO-tee.*

1019. **Lip.** Χείλι. *KHEE-lee.*

1020. **Liver.** Σ(υ)κώτι. *S(ee)KO-tee.*

1021. **Lung.** Πνευμόνι. *pnev-MO-nee.*

1022. **Mouth.** Στόμα. *STO-ma.*

1023. **Muscle.** Μῦς. *mees.*

1024. **Nail.** Νύχι. *NEE-khee.*

1025. **Neck.** Λαιμός. *leh-MOHSS.*

1026. **Nerve.** Νεῦρο. *NEV-ro.*

1027. **Nose.** Μύτη. *MEE-tee.*

1028. **Rib.** Πλευρό. *plev-RO.*

1029. **Shoulder.** Ὦμος. *O-mohss.*

1030. **Right (left) side.** Δεξιά (ἀριστερή) πλευρά.
    ᴛhek-see-AH (ah-ree-steh-REE) plev-RA.

1031. **Skin.** Δέρμα. *ᴛHER-ma.*

1032. **Skull.** Κρανίο. *krah-NEE-o.*

1033. **Spine.** Ράχη. *RA-khee.*

1034. **Stomach.** Στομάχι. *sto-MA-khee.*

1035. **Throat.** Λαιμός. *leh-MOHSS.*

1036. **Thumb.** Ἀντίχειρ. *ahn-DEE-kheer.*

1037. **Toe.** Δάκτυλο τοῦ ποδιοῦ.
    ᴛHA-ktee-lo too po-ᴛHYOO.

1038. **Tongue.** Γλῶσσα. *GHLO-sa.*

1039. **Tonsils.** Ἀμυγδαλές. *ah-meegh-tha-LESS.*

1040. **Tooth.** Δόντι. *ᴛHOHN-dee.*

1041. **Waist.** Μέση. *MEH-see.*

1042. **Wrist.** Καρπός. *kar-POHSS.*

COMMUNICATIONS: TELEPHONE

1045. **Where can I telephone?**

Ποῦ μπορῶ νά τηλεφωνήσω;
POO bo-RO na-tee-le-fo-NEE-so?

1046. Will you telephone for me?

Τηλεφωνεῖτε γιὰ μένα;

tee-le-fo-NEE-teh ya MEH-na?

1047. I want to make a local call, number ———.

Θέλω νὰ κάνω ἕνα τοπικὸ τηλεφώνημα, ἀριθμός ———.

THEH-lo na-KA-no EH-na toh-pee-KO tee-le-FO-nee-mà, ah-reeth-MOHSS ———.

1048. Give me the long distance operator.

Δῶστε μου τὸν τηλεφωνητὴ μακρᾶς ἀποστάσεως.

THO-steh-moo tohn tee-le-fo-nee-TEE ma-KRASS ah-po-STA-seh-ohss.

1049. The operator will call you.

Ὁ τηλεφωνητὴς *m.* (ἡ τηλεφωνήτρια *f.*) θὰ σᾶς καλέση.

o tee-le-fo-nee-TEESS (ee tee-le-fo-NEE-tree-ah) tha sass ka-LESS-ee.

1050. I want number ———.

Θέλω τὸν ἀριθμό ———.

THEH-lo tohn ah-reeth-MO ———.

1051. Hello.

Ἐμπρός.

ehm-BROHSS.

1052. They do not answer.

Δὲν ἀπαντοῦν.

then ah-pahn-DOON.

1053. The line is busy.

Ἡ γραμμή εἶναι ἀπησχοληµένη.

ee ghra-MEE EE-neh ah-peess-kho-lee-MEH-nee.

1054. Hold the line, please.

Κρατεῖστε τὴ γραμμή, παρακαλῶ.

kra-TEESS-teh tee ghra-MEE pah-ra-ka-LO.

1055. May I speak to ——?

Μπορῶ νὰ µιλήσω στὸ *m.* (or στή *f.*) ——;

bo-RO na-mee-LEE-so sto (or stee) ——?

1056. He is not in.

Δὲν εἶναι ἐδῶ.

then EE-neh eh-THO.

1057. This is —— speaking.

Ἐδῶ ——.

eh-THO ——.

1058. Please take a message for ——.

Παρακαλῶ κρατεῖστε σημείωση γιὰ ——.

pa-ra-ka-LO kra-TEE-steh see-MEE-o-see ya ——.

1059. My number is ——.

Ὁ ἀριθμὸς τοῦ τηλεφώνου µου εἶναι ——.

o ah-reeth-MOHSS too tee-le-FO-noo-moo EE-neh ——.

1060. How much is a call to ——?

Πόσο ἔχει ἕνα τηλεφώνημα γιὰ ——;

PO-so EH-khee EH-na tee-le-FO-nee-ma ya ——?

1061. There is a telephone call for you.
Ἔχετε ἕνα τηλεφώνημα.
EH-kheh-teh EH-na tee-le-FO-nee-ma.

USEFUL INFORMATION: DAYS OF THE WEEK

1062. Sunday. Κυριακή. *keer-ya-KEE.*

1063. Monday. Δευτέρα. *ᵗhef-TEH-ra.*

1064. Tuesday. Τρίτη. *TREE-tee.*

1065. Wednesday. Τετάρτη. *teh-TAR-tee.*

1066. Thursday. Πέμπτη. *PEMP-tee.*

1067. Friday. Παρασκευή. *pa-ra-skev-EE.*

1068. Saturday. Σάββατο. *SA-va-to.*

MONTHS, SEASONS, AND WEATHER

1069. January. Ἰανουάριος. *ee-ahn-oo-AR-ee-ohss.*

1070. February. Φεβρουάριος. *fev-roo-AR-ee-ohss.*

1071. March. Μάρτιος. *MAR-tee-ohss.*

1072. April. Ἀπρίλιος. *ah-PREEL-ee-ohss.*

1073. May. Μάϊος. *MA-ee-ohss.*

1074. June. Ἰούνιος. *ee-OON-ee-ohss.*

1075. July. Ἰούλιος. *ee-OOL-ee-ohss.*

1076. August. Αὔγουστος. *AHV-ghoo-stohss.*

1077. September. Σεπτέμβριος. *sep-TEM-vree-ohss.*

1078. October. Ὀκτώβριος. *ohk-TOHV-ree-ohss.*

1079. November. Νοέμβριος. *no-EM-vree-ohss.*

1080. December. Δεκέμβριος. *ᵗheh-KEM-vree-ohss.*

1081. Spring. Άνοιξη. *AH-nee-ksee.*

1082. Summer. Καλοκαίρι. *ka-lo-KEH-ree.*

1083. Fall. Φθινόπωρο. *fthee-NO-po-ro.*

1084. Winter. Χειμώνας. *khee-MO-nass.*

1085. It is warm (cold). Κάνει ζέστη (κρύο).
   KA-nee ZEST-ee (KREE-o).

1086. The weather is good. Ὁ καιρὸς εἶναι καλός.
   o ke-ROHSS EE-neh ka-LOHSS.

1087. The weather is bad. Ὁ καιρὸς δὲν εἶναι καλός.
   o ke-ROHSS then EE-neh ka-LOHSS.

1088. The sun. Ὁ ἥλιος. *o EE-lee-ohs.*

1089. In the shade. Στὴ σκιά. *stee skee-A.*

1090. It is raining. It is snowing.
   Βρέχει. Χιονίζει.
   VRE-khee. khyo-NEE-zee.

HOLIDAYS

1091. Christmas. Χριστούγεννα. *khree-STOO-yen-ah.*

1092. Easter. Πάσχα. *PA-skha.*

1093. Good Friday. Μεγάλη Παρασκευή.
   meh-GHA-lee pa-ra-skev-EE.

1094. Lent. Σαρακοστή. *sa-ra-ko-STEE.*

1095. New Year's Day. Πρωτοχρονιά. *pro-to-khro-NYA.*

1096. Legal holiday. Νομικὴ ἑορτή.
   no-mee-KEE eh-or-TEE.

TIME AND TIME EXPRESSIONS

1097. What time is it?
   Τὶ ὥρα εἶναι;
   TEE OR-ah EE-neh?

1098. It is two o'clock a.m. (p.m.).
Εἶναι δύο π.μ. (μ.μ.).
EE-neh $\overline{THEE}$*-o.*

1099. It is half past six.
Εἶναι ἕξι καὶ μισή.
EE-neh EK-see keh mee-SEE.

1100. It is quarter past two.
Εἶναι δύο καὶ τέταρτο.
EE-neh $\overline{THEE}$*-o keh TEH-tar-toh.*

1101. It is quarter to three.
Εἶναι τρεῖς παρὰ τέταρτο.
EE-neh TREESS pa-ra TEH-tar-toh.

1102. At ten minutes to four.
Στὶς τέσσερες παρὰ δέκα.
steess TEH-ser-ess pa-ra $\overline{THEH}$*-ka.*

1103. At ten minutes past five.
Στὶς πέντε καὶ δέκα.
steess PEN-deh keh $\overline{THEH}$*-ka.*

1105. In the morning.
Τὸ πρωΐ.
toh pro-EE.

1106. In the evening.
Τὸ βράδυ.
*toh VRA-*t̄*hee.*

1107. In the afternoon.   Τὸ ἀπόγευμα.
toh ah-PO-yev̆-ma.

1108. At noon.   Τὸ μεσημέρι.
toh mess-ee-MEH-ree.

1109. Day.   Ἡμέρα.   *ee-MEH-ra.*

1110. Night. Νύκτα. *NEEK-ta.*

1111. Midnight. Μεσάννκτα. *meh-SA-neek-ta.*

1112. Yesterday. Χθές. *khthess.*

1113. Last night. Ψές. *psess.*

1114. Today. Σήμερα. *SEE-meh-ra.*

1115. Tonight. Ἀπόψε. *ah-PO-pseh.*

1116. Tomorrow. Αὔριο. *AHV-ree-o.*

1117. Last year. Πέρυσι. *PEH-ree-see.*

1118. Last month. Τὸν περασμένο μῆνα.
tohn-be-rahz-MEH-no MEE-na.

1119. Next Monday.
Τὴν ἐρχομένη Δευτέρα.
teen er-kho-MEH-nee īhef-TEH-ra.

1120. Next week.
Τὴν ἐρχομένη ἑβδομάδα.
teen er-kho-MEH-nee ev-īho-MA-īha.

1121. The day before yesterday.
Προχθές.
pro-KHTHESS.

1122. The day after tomorrow.
Μεθαύριο.
me-THAV-ree-o.

1123. Two weeks ago.
Πρὸ δύο ἑβδομάδων.
pro THEE-o ev-īho-MA-īhohn.

1124. One week ago.
Πρὸ μιᾶς ἑβδομάδος.
pro mee-ASS ev-īho-MA-īhohss.

NUMBERS: CARDINALS

1125. 1. **One.** Ἕνας *m.*, μία or μιά *f.*, ἕνα *n.*
EH-nass, MEE-ah, EH-na.

2. **Two.** Δύο or δυό. *THEE-o.*

3. **Three.** Τρεῖς *m. f.*, τρία *n.* *TREESS, TREE-ah.*

4. **Four.** Τέσσερεις *m. f.*, τέσσερα *n.*
TEH-seh-reess, TEH-seh-ra.

5. **Five.** Πέντε. *PEN-deh.*

6. **Six.** Ἕξι. *EK-see.*

7. **Seven.** Ἑφτὰ or ἑπτά. *ef-TA.*

8. **Eight.** Ὀχτὼ or ὀκτώ. *okh-TO.*

9. **Nine.** Ἐννέα or ἐννιά. *eh-NEH-a.*

10. **Ten.** Δέκα. *THEH-ka.*

11. **Eleven.** Ἕντεκα. *EHN-deh-ka.*

12. **Twelve.** Δώδεκα. *THO-theh-ka.*

13. **Thirteen.** Δεκατρία. *theh-ka-TREE-a.*

14. **Fourteen.** Δεκατέσσερα. *theh-ka-TEH-seh-ra.*

15. **Fifteen.** Δεκαπέντε. *theh-ka-PEN-deh.*

16. **Sixteen.** Δεκαέξι or δεκάξι. *theh-ka-EK-see.*

17. **Seventeen.** Δεκαεφτά. *theh-ka-ef-TA.*

18. **Eighteen.** Δεκαοχτώ. *theh-ka-okh-TOH.*

19. **Nineteen.** Δεκαεννιά. *theh-ka-eh-NYA.*

20. **Twenty.** Εἴκοσι. *EE-ko-see.*

21. **Twenty-one.** Εἴκοσι ἕνας, εἴκοσι μία, εἴκοσι ἕνα.
EE-ko-see EH-nass, EE-ko-see MEE-ah, EE-ko-see EH-na.

22. **Twenty-two.** Εἴκοσι δύο. *EE-ko-see THEE-o.*

30. **Thirty.** Τριάντα. *tree-AHN-da.*

31. **Thirty-one.** Τριάντα ἕνα. *tree-AHN-da EH-na.*

40. **Forty.** Σαράντα. *sa-RAHN-da.*

50. **Fifty.** Πενήντα. *pen-EEN-da.*

60. **Sixty.** Ἑξήντα. *ek-SEEN-da.*

70. **Seventy.** Ἑβδομήντα. *ev-tho-MEEN-da.*

80. **Eighty.** Ὀγδόντα. *ogh-THOHN-da.*

90. **Ninety.** Ἐνενήντα. *eh-neh-NEEN-da.*

100. **One hundred.** Ἑκατό. *eh-ka-TOH.*

200. **Two hundred.**
Διακόσιοι *m.*, διακόσιες *f.*, διακόσια *n.*
thee-a-KO-see-ee, thee-ah-KO-see-ess, thee-ah-KO-see-a.

1 000. **One thousand.** Χίλιοι *m.*, χίλιες *f.*, χίλια *n.*
KHEE-lee-ee, KHEE-lee-ess, KHEE-lee-ah.

2 000. **Two thousand.** Δύο χιλιάδες.
THEE-o khee-lee-AH-thess.

NUMBERS : ORDINALS

1126. (The ordinal numerals as well as the adjectives have different endings for each of the three genders. They are: -ος for the masculine, -η for the feminine, -ο for the neuter.)

First. Πρῶτος *m.*, πρώτη *f.*, πρῶτο *n.*
PRO-tohss, PRO-tee, PRO-to.

Second. Δεύτερος (*f.* δευτέρα). *THEF-teh-rohss (f.thef-TEH-*
Third. Τρίτος. *TREE-tohss.*   *rah).*

Fourth. Τέταρτος. *TET-ar-tohss.*

Fifth. Πέμπτος. *PEMP-tohss.*

Sixth. Ἕκτος. *EK-tohss.*

Seventh. Ἕβδομος. *EV-tho-mohss.*

Eighth. Ὄγδοος. *OGH-tho-ohss.*

Ninth. Ἔνατος. *EH-na-tohss.*

Tenth. Δέκατος. *THEH-ka-tohss.*

1955. Χίλια ἐννιακόσια πενήντα πέντε.
KHEE-lee-a eh-nya-KO-sya pen-EEN-da PEN-deh.

MEASUREMENTS

1127. What is the length (width)?
Ποῖο εἶναι τὸ μῆκος (πλάτος);
PEE-o EE-neh toh MEE-kohss (PLA-tohss)?

1128. How much is it per meter?

Πόσο ἔχει τὸ μέτρο;

PO-so EH-khee toh MET-ro?

1129. What is the size?

Ποῖο εἶναι τὸ μέγεθος;

PEE-o EE-neh toh MEH-yeh-thohss?

1130. It is ten meters long by four meters wide.

Ἔχει δέκα μέτρα μῆκος τέσσερα μέτρα πλάτος.

EH-khee $\overline{THEH}$-ka MET-ra MEE-kohss TEH-seh-ra MET-ra PLA-tohss.

1131. High.   (Ὑ)Ψηλό.   *(ee)-psee-LO.*

1132. Low.   Χαμηλό.   *kha-mee-LO.*

1133. Large.   Μεγάλο.   *meh-GHA-lo.*

1134. Small.   Μικρό.   *mee-KRO.*

1135. Medium.   Μέτριο.   *MET-ree-o.*

1136. Alike.   Τὸ ἴδιο.   *toh-EE-$\overline{thee}$-o.*

1137. Different.   Διαφορετικό.

$\overline{thee}$-ah-fo-reh-tee-KO.

1138. A pair.   Ζεῦγος.   *ZEV-ghohss.*

1139. A dozen.   Μιὰ ντοζίνα or δωδεκάδα.

mya doo-ZEE-na or $\overline{tho}$-$\overline{theh}$-KA-$\overline{tha}$.

1140. Half a dozen.   Μισὴ ντοζίνα.

mee-SEE doo-ZEE-na.

1141. Half a meter.   Μισὸ μέτρο.

mee-SO MET-ro.

COLORS

1143. Light. 'Ανοικτό. *ah-neek-TOH.*

1144. Dark. Σκοῦρο. *SKOO-ro.*

1145. Black. Μαῦρο. *MAHV-ro.*

1146. Blue. Μπλέ. *BLEH.*

1147. Brown. Καφέ. *ka-FEH.*

1148. Cream. Κρέμ. *KREHM.*

1149. Gray. Γκρί. *GREE.*

1150. Green. Πράσινο. *PRA-see-no.*

1151. Orange. Πορτοκαλί. *port-o-ka-LEE.*

1152. Pink. Ρόζ. *ROHZ.*

1153. Purple. Μώβ. *MOHV.*

1154. Red. Κόκκινο. *KO-kee-no.*

1155. White. Άσπρο. *ASP-ro.*

1156. Yellow. Κίτρινο. *KEE-tree-no.*

1157. I want a lighter (darker) shade.
Θέλω πιό ἀνοικτό (σκοῦρο).
THEH-lo pyo ah-neek-TOH (SKOO-ro).

COMMON OBJECTS

1160. Ash tray. Τασάκι. *ta-SA-kee.*

1161. Bobby pins. Τσιμπιδάκια γιά τά μαλλιά.
tseem-bee-THA-kya ya ta ma-LYA.

1162. Bottle opener. 'Ανοιχτήρι (μπουκαλιῶν).
ah-neekh-TEE-ree (boo-ka-LYOHN).

1163. Box. Κάσα, κιβώτιο, or κουτί.
KA-sa, kee-VO-tee-o, or koo-TEE.

1164. Bulb (light). Γλόμπος. *GHLOHM-bohss.*

1165. Candy. Ζαχαρωτά. *za-kha-ro-TA.*

1166. Can opener. 'Ανοιχτήρι (κονσερβῶν).
 ah-neekh-TEE-ree (kohn-ser-VOHN).

1167. Cleaning fluid. (Benzine.) Βενζίνη. *ven-ZEE-nee.*

1168. Cloth. Ὕφασμα. *EE-faz-ma.*

1169. Clock. Ρολόϊ. *ro-LO-ee.*

1170. Cork. Φελλός. *feh-LOSS.*

1171. Corkscrew. Τιρμπουσόνι. *teer-boo-SO-nee.*

1172. Doll. Κούκλα. *KOO-kla.*

1173. Earrings. Σκουλαρίκια. *skoo-la-REE-kya.*

1174. Flashlight. Φακός or κλεφτοφάναρο.
 fa-KOHSS or klef-toh-FA-na-ro.

1175. Glasses. Γυαλιά. *ya-LYA.*

1176. Sunglasses. Γυαλιά τοῦ ἡλίου.
 ya-LYA too ee-LEE-oo.

1177. Gold. Χρυσός. *khree-SOHSS.*

1178. Chewing gum. Μαστίχα. *mass-TEE-kha.*
 Chiclets. Τσίχλες. *TSEEKH-less.*

1179. Hairnet. Δίχτυ γιὰ τὰ μαλλιὰ or φιλέ.
 $\overline{T}HEEKH$-tee ya tah ma-LYA or fee-LEH.

1180. Hook. Κρεμάστρα. *kreh-MASS-tra.*

1181. Iron (flat). Σίδερο (σιδερώματος).
 SEE-the-ro (see-$\overline{th}$eh-RO-ma-tohss).

1182. Jewelry. Κοσμήματα or διαμαντικά.
 kohz-MEE-ma-ta or $\overline{th}$ee-ah-mahn-dee-KA.

1183. Leather. Δέρμα or πετσί. $\overline{T}HER$-ma or pet-SEE.

1184. Linen. Λινά. *lee-NA.*

1185. Lock. Κλειδωνιά. *klee-tho-NYA.*

1186. Mirror. Καθρέφτης. *ka-THREF-teess.*

1187. Mosquito net. Κουνουπιέρα. *koo-noo-PYER-ah.*

1188. Necklace. Περιδέραιο. per-ee-$\overline{T}HER$-eh-o.

1189. Needle. Βελόνι. *veh-LO-nee.*

1190. Notebook. Σημειωματάριο. *see-mee-o-ma-TAR-ee-o.*

1191. Pail. Κουβάς. *koo-VASS.*

1192. **Penknife.** Σουγιάς. *soo-YASS.*

1193. **Perfume.** Μυρωδιά. *mee-ro-THYA.*

1194. **Pillow.** Μαξιλάρι. *ma-ksee-LA-ree.*

1195. **Pin (ornamental).** Καρφίτσα. *kar-FEE-tsa.*

1196. **Pin (safety).** Παραμάνα. *pa-ra-MA-na.*

1197. **Pin (straight).** Καρφίτσα. *kar-FEE-tsa.*

1198. **Purse.** Πορτοφόλι. *port-o-FO-lee.*

1199. **Radio.** Ραδιόφωνο. *rah-thee-O-fo-no.*

1200. **Ring.** Δαχτυλίδι. *tha-khtee-LEE-thee.*

1201. **Rubbers.** Γαλότσες. *gha-LO-tsess.*

1202. **Scissors.** Ψαλίδι. *psa-LEE-thee.*

1203. **Screw.** Βίδα. *VEE-tha.*

1204. **Sheet.** Σεντόνι. *sen-DOH-nee.*

1205. **Shoelaces.** Κορδόνια. *kor-THO-nya.*

1206. **Silk.** Μετάξι. *meh-TA-ksee.*

1207. **Silver.** 'Ασήμι. *ah-SEE-mee.*

1208. **(Precious) stone.** (Πολύτιμη) πέτρα. *(po-LEE-tee-mee) PET-ra.*

1209. **Stopper.** Βούλωμα. *VOO-lι-ma.*

1210. **Strap.** Λωρί. *lo-REE.*

1211. **Straw.** Ψάθινο καπέλο. *PSA-thee-no ka-PEL-o.*

1212. **Suitcase.** Βαλίτσα. *va-LEE-tsa.*

1213. **Thimble.** Δαχτυλίθρα. *tha-khtee-LEE-thra.*

1214. **Thread.** Κλωστή. *kloss-TEE.*

1215. **Typewriter.** Γραφομηχανή. *ghra-fo-mee-kha-NEE.*

1216. **Umbrella.** 'Ομπρέλα. *ohm-BREL-ah.*

1217. **Vase.** Βάζο. *VA-zo.*

1218. **Watch.** Ρολόϊ. *ro-LO-ee.*

1219. **Whiskbroom.** Σκουπίτσα. *skoo-PEE-tsa.*

1220. **Wire.** Σύρμα. *SEER-ma.*

1221. **Wood.** Ξύλο. *KSEE-lo.*

1222. **Wool.** Μαλλί. *ma-LEE.*

1223. **Zipper.** Φορμουάρ. *form-oo-AR.*

FOOD

(This food list has been alphabetized according to the Greek names of the food listed in order to facilitate the tourist's reading of Greek menus.)

1224. Artichokes. Ἀγκινάρες. *ahn-gee-NA-ress.*

1225. Cucumber. Ἀγγούρι. *ahn-GOO-ree.*

1226. Almond cookies. Ἀμυγδαλωτά. *ah-meegh-tha-lo-TA.*

1227. Spit-roasted lamb. Ἀρνὶ τῆς σούβλας.
ar-NEE teess SOOV-lass.

1228. Lobster. Ἀστακός. *ah-sta-KOHSS.*

1229. Eggs (soft boiled, hard boiled).
Αὐγὰ (μελάτα, σφιχτά).
av-GHA (mel-AH-ta, sfeekh-TAH).

1230. Eggs poached. Αὐγὰ βρασμένα μάτια.
av-GHA vraz-MEH-na MA-tya.

1231. Eggs (fried, scrambled).
Αὐγὰ (τηγανιτά, ἀνακατεμένα).
av-GHA (tee-gha-nee-TA, ah-na-ka-teh-MEH-na).

1232. Lemon and egg sauce. Αὐγολέμονο.
av-gho-LEH-mo-no.

1233. Pears. Ἀχλάδια. *akh-LA-thya.*

1234. Apricots. Βερίκοκκα. *veh-REE-ko-ka.*

1235. Milk. Γάλα. *GHA-la.*

1236. Milk-pie. Γαλατόπιτα. *gha-la-TO-pee-ta.*

1237. Turkey. Γαλοπούλα. *gha-lo-POO-la.*

1238. Shrimps. Γαρίδες. *gha-REE-thess.*

1239. Yogurt. Γιαούρτι. *ya-OOR-tee.*

1240. Dessert. Γλύκισμα. *GHLEE-keez-ma.*

1241. Jam. Γλυκὸ τοῦ κουταλιοῦ.
ghlee-KO too koo-ta-LEW.

1242. Olives. Ἐλιές. *eh-LYES.*

1243. Ham and eggs. Ζαμπὸν μὲ αὐγά.
zahm-BOHN meh av-GHA.

1244. (Chicken) broth. (Κότας) ζωμός.
(*KO-tass*) *zo-MOHSS.*

1245. Cold eggplant stuffed with vegetables.
Ἰμάμ μπαϊλντί. *ee-MAM bah-eel-DEE.*

1246. Crabs. Καβούρια. *ka-VOOR-ya.*

1247. Shredded wheat biscuit with nuts and syrup.
Κανταΐφι. *kahn-da-EE-fee.*

1248. Stew. Καπαμάς. *ka-pa-MASS.*

1249. Carrots. Καρότα. *ka-RO-ta.*

1250. Watermelon. Καρπούζι. *kar-POO-zee.*

1251. Nuts (walnuts). Καρύδια. *ka-REE-thya.*

1252. Chestnuts. Κάστανα. *KASS-ta-na.*

1253. Black coffee. Καφές. *ka-FESS.*

1254. Coffee (with milk, cream).
Καφὲς (μὲ γάλα, κρέμα).
ka-FESS (meh GHA-la, KREH-ma).

1255. Cherries. Κεράσια. *keh-RA-sya.*

1256. Meat balls. Κεφτέδες. *kef-TEH-thess.*

1257. Chopped meat. Κιμάς. *kee-MASS.*

1258. Beets. Κοκκινογούλια. *ko-kee-no-GHOO-lya.*

1259. Roasted intestines wound on a spit. Κοκορέτσι.
ko-ko-RET-see.

1260. Squash. Κολοκυθάκια. *ko-lo-kee-THA-kya.*

1261. Pumpkin-pie. Κολοκυθόπιτα.
ko-lo-kee-THO-pee-ta.

1262. Stewed fruit. Κομπόστα. *kom-BO-sta.*

1263. Chicken (roast, fried).
Κότα (ψητή, τηγανιτή).
KO-ta (psee-TEE, tee-gha-nee-TEE).

1264. Chicken rice soup with eggs and lemon.
Κότα σούπα αὐγολέμονο.
KO-ta SOO-pa av-gho-LEH-mo-no.

1265. Rabbit. Κουνέλι. *koo-NEL-ee.*

1266. Cauliflower. Κουνουπίδι. *koo-noo-PEE-thee.*

1267. Greek cookies. Κουραμπιέδες. *koo-rahm-BYEH-thess.*

1268. Meat. Κρέας. *KREH-ass.*

1269. Onion. Κρεμμύδι. *kreh-MEE-thee.*

1270. Hare stew. Λαγὸς στιφάδο. *la-GHOSS stee-FA-thoh.*

1271. Green vegetables. Λαχανικά. *la-kha-nee-KA.*

1272. Cabbage. (Καρμπο) λάχανο. *(kar-bo-) LA-kha-no.*

1273. Lemonade. Λεμονάδα. *leh-mo-NA-tha.*

1274. Lemon. Λεμόνι. *leh-MO-nee.*

1275. Sausage. Λουκάνικο. *loo-KA-nee-ko.*

1276. Fritters like doughnuts (with honey).
Λουκομάδες. *loo-ko-MA-thess.*

1277. Giblet soup with eggs and lemon. Μαγειρίτσα.
ma-yee-REE-tsa.

1278. Mushrooms. Μανιτάρια. *ma-nee-TAR-ya.*

1279. Lettuce. Μαρούλι. *ma-ROO-lee.*

1280. Eggplants (stuffed). Μελιτζάνες (γεμιστές).
meh-leed-ZA-ness (yeh-mee-STESS).

1281. Eggplants and meat in tomato sauce.
Μελιτζάνες μουσακά. *meh-leed-ZA-ness moo-sa-KA.*

1282. Apple. Μῆλο. *MEE-lo.*

1283. Veal (cutlet). Μοσχάρι (κοτολέτα).
moss-KHA-ree (ko-to-LET-ah).

1284. Mustard. Μουστάρδα. *moo-STAR-tha.*

1285. Codfish fried. Μπακαλιάρος (τηγανιτός).
ba-ka-LYA-rohss (tee-gha-nee-TOHSS).

1286. Baklava. Μπακλαβάς. *ba-kla-VASS.*

1287. Okra. Μπάμιες. *BA-myes.*

1288. Bananas. Μπανάνες. *ba-NA-ness.*

1289. Peas. Μπιζέλια. *bee-ZEH-lya.*

1290. Chops. Μπριτζόλες. *breed-ZO-less.*

1291. Beef steak. Μπιφτέκι. *beef-TEH-kee.*

1292. Brains. Μυαλά. *mya-LA.*

1293. **Stuffed vine leaves.** Ντολμάδες or σαρμάδες.
  dohl-MA-thess or *sar-MA-thess.*

1294. **Tomatoes (stuffed).** Ντομάτες (γεμιστές).
  do-MA-tess (yeh-mee-STESS).

1295. **Hors-d'œuvre.** 'Ορεκτικά. *o-reh-ktee-KA.*

1296. **Omelette.** 'Ομελέτα. *o-meh-LET-ah.*

1297. **Ice cubes.** Μικρά κομμάτια πάγου.
  meek-RA ko-MA-tya PA-ghoo.

1298. **Ice cream** or **custard.** Παγωτό. *pa-gho-TOH.*

1299. **Duck.** Πάπια. *PA-pya.*

1300. **Cake.** Πάστα. *PASS-ta.*

1301. **A dish of macaroni and chopped meat.** Παστίτσιο.
  pa-STEE-tsyo.

1302. **Partridge.** Πέρδικα. *PER-thee-ka.*

1303. **Rice and meat.** Πιλάφι. *pee-LA-fee.*

1304. **Potatoes (boiled, baked, fried).**
  Πατάτες (βρασμένες, ψημένες, τηγανιτές).
  *pa-TA-tess   (vraz-MEH-ness,   psee-MEH-ness,
  tee-gha-nee-TESS).*

1305. **Potatoes (mashed).** Πατάτες (πουρέ).
  pa-TA-tess (poo-REH).

1306. **Tripe.** Πατσάς. *pa-TSASS.*

1307. **Peppers (stuffed).** Πεπεριές (γεμιστές).
  peh-per-YES (yeh-mee-STESS).

1308. **Melon.** Πεπόνι. *peh-PO-nee.*

1309. **Orange juice.** Πορτοκαλάδα. *por-toh-ka-LA-tha.*

1310. **Orange.** Πορτοκάλι. *por-toh-KA-lee.*

1311. **Pudding.** Πουτίγκα. *poo-TEEN-ga.*

1312. **Mutton.** Πρόβειο. *PRO-vyo.*

1313. **Radishes.** Ρεπάνια. *reh-PA-nya.*

1314. **Peaches.** Ροδάκινα. *ro-THA-keen-ah.*

1315. **Roast beef.** Ροσμπίφ. *roz-BEEF.*

1316. **Salami.** Σαλάμι. *sa-LA-mee.*

13i7. Salad. Σαλάτα. *sa-LA-ta.*

1318. Sauce. Σάλτσα. *SAL-tsa.*

1319. Sardine. Σαρδέλα. *sar-$\overline{THEH}$-la.*

1320. Sherbet. Σερμπέτι. *ser-BET-ee.*

1321. Syrup. Σιρόπι. *see-RO-pee.*

1322. Garlic and vinegar sauce (often used with fried codfish).
Σκορδαλιά. *skor-$\overline{tha}$-LYA.*

1323. Garlic. Σκόρδο. *SKOR-$\overline{tho}$.*

1324. Spleens in intestines wound on a spit.
Σπληνάντερο. *spleen-AHN-der-o.*

1325. Salmon. Σολομός. *so-lo-MOHSS.*

1326. Soup. Σούπα. *SOO-pa.*

1327. Spinach. Σπανάκι. *spa-NA-kee.*

1328. Asparagus. Σπαράγγι. *spar-AHN-gee.*

1329. Raisins. Σταφίδες. *sta-FEE-thess.*

1330. Grapes. Σταφύλια. *sta-FEE-lya.*

1331. Oysters. Στρείδια. *STREE-$\overline{thya}$.*

1332. Figs. Σύκα. *SEE-ka.*

1333. Liver. Σ(υ)κώτι. *S(ee)KO-tee.*

1334. Tarama caviar appetizer. Ταραμοσαλάτα.
ta-ra-mo-sa-LA-ta.

1335. Pickles. Τουρσί. *toor-SEE.*

1336. Tea. Τσάϊ. *TSA-ee.*

1337. Cheese. Τυρί. *tee-REE.*

1338. Cheese-pie. Τυρόπιτα. *tee-RO-pee-ta.*

1339. Lentils. Φακή. *fa-KEE.*

1340. Stringbeans. Φασολάκια. *fa-so-LA-kya.*

1341. Beans. Φασόλια. *fa-SO-lya.*

1342. Bean soup with tomato. Φασολάδα. *fa-so-LA-$\overline{tha}$.*

1343. Strawberries. Φράουλες. *FRA-oo-less.*

1344. Grapefruit. Φράπα. *FRA-pa.*

1345. **Toast and jelly.** Φρυγανιὰ μὲ μαρμελάδα.
free-gha-NYA meh mar-mel-AH-tha.

1346. **Pork.** Χοίρινο. *KHEE-ree-no.*

1347. **Pork with beans.** Χοίρινο μὲ φασόλια.
KHEE-ree-no meh fa-SO-lya.

1348. **Pork chops (fried).**
Χοίρινες μπριτζόλες (τηγανιτές).
KHEE-ree-ness breed-ZO-less (tee-gha-nee-TESS).

1349. **Fish.** Ψάρι. *PSA-ree.*

1350. **Fish boiled with mayonnaise.**
Ψάρι βραστὸ μὲ μαγιονέζα.
PSA-ree vrass-TO meh mah-yon-EH-za.

1351. **Fish soup.** Ψάρι σούπα or ψαρόσουπα.
PSA-ree SOO-pa or psa-RO-soo-pa.

1352. **Fish fried.** Ψάρια τηγανιτά.
PSA-rya tee-gha-nee-TA.

1353. **Rolls and butter.** Ψωμάκια καὶ βούτυρο.
pso-MA-kya keh VOO-tee-ro.

1354. **Bread.** Ψωμί. *pso-MEE.*

INDEX

The words in CAPITALS refer to sections, and the first number that follows (example: p. 98) refers to the page. Otherwise, ALL ENTRIES ARE INDEXED BY ITEM NUMBER.